I am excited to endorse Leanna Brewer's new book, *She Shepherd*. This book empowers women to use their voice, take their God-given place, breathe life into dreams that have died, and change the world around them. Leanna has captured the heart of God as a mother, minister, and bold risk-taker, setting women free to walk as daughters of the King of kings and fulfill their destiny on this earth. *She Shepherd* inspires you to have a new image of yourself and shatter doubts from past mistakes that tell you to give up. Thank you, Leanna Brewer, for writing such a powerful and encouraging book that unlocks potential, new vision, and advancement for women to take their place in powerful leadership positions.

Cindy McGill
Author of *Words That Work, Methods That End the Madness* and
What Your Dreams Are Telling You
Hope for the Harvest Ministries
www.cindymcgill.org

Leanna Brewer is a woman I highly look up to, and when I hear her testify, it's contagious and gets all over me. She not only lives the great commission, but when you get in her orbit, you get sucked into the red letter words of Jesus. This book is a standard bearer for women today. She has brought Heaven to earth and delivers language to us everyday women to see how we also love this abundant life Jesus paid for without hindrance! This is a must-read, ladies! Five stars.

Jamie Lyn Wallnau
Wife, Mother, Author, Host of *Set Apart Women* Podcast

Few recognize the profound risk Ruth undertook when she approached Boaz that fateful night. By stepping into the unknown, she placed her very life on the line, embodying a profound understanding of her God-given identity. In our contemporary world, we face a pervasive identity crisis, a perilous void in self-awareness and purpose. This crisis is particularly alarming as we desperately need strong, unwavering individuals to bridge the gap for the next generation. Leanna Brewer's new book, *She Shepherd,* emerges as a powerful balm for these identity wounds, offering weighty insights and inspiration that will help you reclaim your true identity in Christ. Don't just read this book—share it and pray that God will raise up more she shepherds in this hour!

Alan DiDio
Host of *Encounter Today*
Pastor of The Encounter Charlotte

Dr. Leanna Brewer's book, *She Shepherd,* is a fresh and enlightened perspective on the beauty of a life dedicated to God. You will enjoy her personal stories and reflections of how God met her along the way to grow and mature her into the amazing ministry leader she is today. If you need encouragement and guidance to hear God's process of promotion as He molds and shapes you into the likeness of His Son, Jesus, this book is for you. Dr. Leanna's own courage and authenticity will spark you to continue the process forward until you reach your destiny, too.

Dr. Candice Smithyman
Host, *Glory Road* TV Show, Author, Speaker
www.candicesmithyman.com

Leanna Brewer's book, *She Shepherd,* is a tent peg of truth to the lies women believe about themselves. The book is packed full of Holy Spirit insight, compelling personal stories, and wisdom that only comes from conforming your life to God's plan. Leanna is transparent, authentic, and a spiritual mama to many! I can't recommend this book enough!

JerriAnn Webb
Founder, Light Breaks Through
Author of *Heaven in My Home* and *The Kingdom*
Executive Producer, *Repair the Breach* Movie

Leanna Brewer doesn't just talk the talk—she walks the walk, spreading Christ's love through outrageously generous acts of mercy. *She Shepherd* is a testament to this kindness, delivering a raw, inspiring journey of faith and personal growth. This book is a must-read for anyone looking to live a life drenched in love and compassion.

Darren Stott
Senior Leader, Eden Church

I have had the privilege of endorsing a lot of books over the past few years. This is one I cannot mess up for obvious reasons. Leanna Brewer is the single most selfless person I have ever known outside of her mama. I knew Leanna as a beautiful teenage girl, and now I know her as she pushes me over the 60-year-old mark.

I have seen her joyous, strong, and full of Spirit-filled faith while suffering through building a church, having a machine gun pointed at her, giving birth, and patiently dealing with my growth and learning curve. All of them were equally horrifying.

Now, she writes her first book and comes out of the chute armed to the teeth with how she carries Jesus. She's something else. Leanna is a true pastor with the heart of a shepherd. She is the love of my life and the greatest influencer of the Kingdom in my entire Christian experience. She's a good girl. Really. Excellent behavior and not to be trifled with.

Troy Brewer
Dr. Leanna Brewer's husband since 1989

LEANNA BREWER, DMIN

She SHEPHERD

**Positioning Yourself for Promotion
from the Field to the Palace**

DESTINY IMAGE® PUBLISHERS, INC.

P.O. Box 310, Shippensburg, PA 17257-0310

"Publishing cutting-edge prophetic resources to supernaturally empower the body of Christ"

This book and all other Destiny Image and Destiny Image Fiction books are available at Christian bookstores and distributors worldwide.

For more information on foreign distributors, call 717-532-3040.

Reach us on the Internet: www.destinyimage.com.

ISBN 13 TP: 979-8-8815-0227-0

ISBN 13 eBook: 979-8-8815-0228-7

For Worldwide Distribution, Printed in the U.S.A.

1 2 3 4 5 6 7 8 / 28 27 26 25 24

Dedication

I dedicate this, my very first book, to my Lord and Savior, Jesus Christ, as my first fruit offering. There are some very special people in my life that I considered dedicating this book to, including my mother, Mary Knight, and my mentor and hero, Pastor Gloria Gillespie, but I chose instead to dedicate it to my very best Friend, the Lover of my soul and heart, Jesus. May it glorify You in every way!

Jesus, I love You most,

Leanna

Contents

Foreword

by
Patricia King

Leanna Brewer is truly one of my "SHEROES"! From the first time I met Leanna, I knew I had come face-to-face with a woman of sincere love, compassion, and mercy, in addition to unwavering faith, commitment, and loyalty—a true Proverbs 31 woman! When you are in her presence, you are encouraged to know that all things are possible in God and that whatever you are facing, all will work out for good and glory!

As I started reading her book, *She Shepherd,* I was reminded of some of the precious stories she shared with me about her upbringing. With very humble beginnings and hearts filled with love for the oppressed, abandoned, and abused, her family unselfishly became the hands and feet of Jesus to many the Lord brought into their home.

When you read *She Shepherd,* you will discover a plumb line example for authentic Christian life. God is calling those who are completely sold out to His purposes and mission on earth.

Leanna's family learned the power of laying down their lives for others. This is what Jesus did for all of us. He did not come to be served but to serve. He was clothed with humility as He laid down His life to serve the needs of mankind. Jesus was rejected, abandoned, slandered, and misrepresented, but continued to love without condition.

Leaving Gethsemane, His illegal trial, false witnesses testifying against Him, mocking, scourging, and brutal beatings, Jesus carried a heavy wooden cross that was heaved onto His back. Weakened with pain, He staggered up to Calvary's hill. An angry mob followed Him, mocking, ridiculing, and shouting, "Crucify Him, crucify Him." They nailed His hands and feet to the cross and hung Him between two guilty criminals. They were crucifying an innocent man.

To many, it looked like Jesus's life was being taken. It appeared that Jesus was defeated, but His life wasn't taken—*it was given!* The devil did not take Jesus's life. The false witnesses did not take His life. The Jews did not kill Him. The Romans did not kill Him. You did not kill Him. No one killed Him. He freely gave His life. When you see Jesus hanging on the cross, you see Love Himself hanging there—a free gift of love—love that had been completely proven and tested against everything that could possibly oppose or destroy it.

Love Himself was on that cross, stripped naked and humiliated, hanging there in agonizing pain. Amid His agony, one of the thieves asked to be saved. Jesus didn't hesitate. In His greatest point of need, He continued to pour Himself out. He could have said, "What do you mean, you want a favor from Me? Really? I don't deserve to be here, and you do. Forget it, it's too late!" Jesus wasn't and isn't like that. He proved His love once again, "Of course, I will save you. In fact, today I'll do it and you will be with Me in paradise. You will see the glory of My salvation."

Looking down from His Cross, Jesus saw a mass of people—a crowd who delighted to watch Him die. "If You're the Son of God, come down off that cross and save Yourself." His merciful, loving retaliation was, *"Father, forgive them; for they do not know what they are doing"* (Luke 23:34).

Can you imagine? We sometimes find it difficult to forgive those who hurt or offend us. Consider Jesus: a mass of angry people rallied against Him, and you were there, too—all humanity was. Oh yes, He saw your face in the crowd that day. We all sinned against Him and yet He said, "Father, forgive them all." He forgave all the sins of mankind right at that point. He cancelled the debt of sin. Only pure Love Himself can do that.

He went even further and actually became mankind's sin. Jesus chose to have your sin poured into Him so He could pour His righteousness into you. He chose to become something abhorrent that would be judged so you would be free from judgment.

Have you ever been mistreated, taken advantage of, or sinned against? Doesn't it give you a great feeling to see the offender punished, knowing they're getting what they deserve? But Jesus's heart was different. He said, "No, I'll take the punishment for your sin. I'll take full responsibility. You can go free."

A number of years ago I was on the mission field. I misjudged a particular situation and consequently made some bad decisions. My actions seriously hurt some individuals. When I finally saw the situation clearly I was terribly grieved, overwhelmed, and deeply ashamed. I thought, *I should have known better, I shouldn't have done that.* It was difficult for me to believe that I hadn't seen the situation through eyes of wisdom in the first place. I asked for forgiveness from one individual who was particularly wounded through the process. The person refused to extend the undeserved mercy that I desperately needed. For years afterward, I had a very difficult time forgiving myself.

One day, I was crying out to the Lord in prayer, "Don't let my failure continue to hurt them. Don't let it ruin their lives." I felt terrible to the very core of my being.

The Lord spoke very soberly to me, "You didn't commit that sin. You didn't make that mistake. I did."

"What? No, Lord! You never did that. I'm the one who did it."

"I did it," He insisted.

"Jesus, no You didn't. You are perfect and You have never wronged anyone, ever!"

He tenderly responded, "I bore your sin on the Cross two thousand years ago. I chose to take full responsibility for this transgression so that you might go free. I have even borne the judgment for it. You are free! I became this sin for you and in exchange I have given you My righteousness. This has all been paid in full. If there is any further problem, that hurting individual will need to come to Me. You have been totally released and fully justified. You never did it!"

I burst into tears of gratitude that flowed from deep inside my being. How can I not love the God who showed that much mercy? He clearly revealed to me that day that this is what He's done for us all. This is what is called "substitution." He literally took our judgment, and in exchange gave us His life and righteousness. Oh my, can we fully grasp this?

God's love for us today is no different from how it was for the sinful crowd at the foot of the Cross two thousand years ago. He performed an eternal exchange, saying, "It is no longer you who sinned, but Me. I have become your sin. I have paid the penalty. I have taken full responsibility. It is no longer your issue." Love laid down His life for all people. Love laid down His life for you! You are free!

Gazing at you through the portals of time, Jesus died on the Cross in love and in faith. He gave up the ghost and cried out, "It is finished." He entrusted His life into the hands of His Father. He died, was buried, and then on the third day He arose from the grave after fully overcoming sin, death, and hell. He has ascended into Heaven and is now seated at the right hand of the Father in glory.

Oh this beautiful Gospel! What a gift! What selfless love! His sacrifice created a reward of exaltation where His name is above every name. As King of kings for all eternity, He is seated on the throne far above all principality, dominion, and rule. Of the increase of His government there shall be no end.

His love, humility, and obedience was modeled for us while He lived on earth. He was and is the message. You have been called for such a time as this to be "Jesus with skin on." I mentioned earlier that Leanna Brewer is one of my "Sheroes," and this is why—she is truly, "Jesus with skin on." Her life is dedicated to this glorious Gospel as she relentlessly serves the poor, children at risk, and beautifully nurtures those the Lord entrusts to her.

Her book *She Shepherd*, will call your heart to journey with Jesus into an exploration of His love and the great commissioning of His glorious Gospel. He has a unique mission for you and this book might just be the very tool you need to hear His clarion call for your life.

Introduction

You may be wondering where in the world I came up with the title of this book. Let me tell you about that.

I absolutely love being in the villages in every country I visit. I love the village. I love the village people, love the village culture and being around animals and nature—and I love the laid-backness. I love all those things about the village. I also appreciate the city. I grew up in that, so I appreciate cities, but I prefer to be in the village, with peace and quietness.

One day I was out in the villages in Uganda with a good friend and sister, Peace Ruharuza. We were walking in the village, looking at the farmland and the agriculture that we were growing to feed the people there. We feed our children we are taking care of and the other families and people in the area. My favorite thing to wear is my overalls, and I wear them when I travel abroad; you will usually find me in a ball cap and overalls because that's my "outfit of choice."

We were walking along, and since I do love animals, I was always stopping and petting some of the farm animals. Peace turned around, looked at me, and started laughing. She said, "Sister, you look like a she shepherd." As soon as she said it, I instantly knew that was going to be the title of the book God had been telling me to write.

I told her I was going to coin that phrase and write a book titled *She Shepherd*. She kind of laughed and looked at me like she didn't think I was actually going to do it, but I obviously did.

To me, the title *She Shepherd* is my life. It is part of what makes me who I am. It is who I am, loving what I do, and being authentically me. I think all of us should be who we are. God only made one of each of us. He only made one of you, so you should be yourself; everyone else is taken. I want to encourage you to seek out who you are and be okay with that.

She Shepherd was a funny title because, in Uganda, women do not become shepherds. That seems odd because the job of a shepherd is to watch over a group of animals. They see to their needs, keep them on the right path, and keep them healthy as they raise them. The Lord has definitely given me the heart to serve, protect, and raise all the kids He has given to me.

Life is different for women in Uganda. Because of the history and culture there, women do just about anything that needs to be done. There aren't exclusively "girl" jobs or "boy" jobs. Everybody pulls together. Yet to be called a she shepherd was really funny to everybody because the only job you do not see women doing there is herding the animals. It's just not something women do.

Women farm, and you can see them out riding on tractors, they are cobblers, they make sheds, they work in the fields, they build houses, they do it all. But I have never—in all my 30-something years of going to Uganda—seen a woman herding animals. So, they thought my "nickname" was really funny. I took it as a great compliment, and I claimed that title and made it my own. I am called "She Shepherd" there.

As the Lord has brought me through all the seasons of my life, He has used me to nurture and raise people. He anointed me to be a mom to our four children, and then He called me to be a mom to shepherd His kids around the world who needed a family.

In this new season, God has grown me and brought me into the position of pastor at OpenDoor Church. It has always puzzled me that many "religious" people in the church have a doctrinal rule that women can't be pastors. When He walked on the earth, Jesus certainly called the women who served around Him into that role. I love that He has anointed me to be the "mamma of the house" at OpenDoor and to be a pastor in His church. So, I see myself as a She Shepherd here, too.

The subtitle of the book, *Positioning Yourself for Promotion from the Field to the Palace,* comes from my favorite story in the Bible, the story of Ruth and Boaz. It is a story of redemption and of the redeemer.

The greatest part of that story is Ruth's faithfulness. Her undying love, her undying dedication, her steadfastness, her ability to lay down her life. She laid it all aside because she truly loved. She truly believed that God was good and that He was calling her to be her mother-in-law's daughter. She did that; she laid it all down when it wasn't easy, and wasn't fun, when her mother-in-law was sad, when the culture was different. When everything was against her, she did everything that her mother-in-law told her.

She went into the fields and worked as a slave, as the poorest of the poor. She had to go glean in the corners of the fields after all the harvesters had finished. She worked hard, and, like Queen Esther, she had a beautiful attitude.

It is one thing to work hard and trust and believe in God, but if you have a stinking attitude, it doesn't glorify God, and it doesn't promote you. She was promoted, just like Queen Esther was, from the field to the palace.

That field seemed to own her at one time in her life. It was where she worked as a slave, but when she was redeemed by the great redeemer, she then owned the field. So she went from that field to the palace. She never lost her grace; she never lost who she was; she never lost her loveliness; she never lost her ability to be the woman God made her be. She was filled with joy, and peace, meekness and humility and loveliness.

This story that plainly shows a shadow of Jesus Himself as the Redeemer is my favorite story. That's why we call the book *She Shepherd: Positioning Yourself for Promotion from the Field to the Palace.*

SECTION ONE

In the Beginning

*Formed in My Mother's Womb
for Such a Time as This*

You formed my innermost being,

shaping my delicate inside and my intricate outside,

and wove them all together in my mother's womb.

I thank you, God, for making me so mysteriously complex!

Everything you do is marvelously breathtaking.

It simply amazes me to think about it!

How thoroughly you know me, Lord!

You even formed every bone in my body

when you created me in the secret place;

carefully skillfully you shaped me

from nothing to something.

You saw who you created me to be

before I became me!

Psalm 139:13-16 TPT

1

Leanna's Childhood

My parents had five biological children. Before I was even born, they were taking in foster children, but not just foster kids. They took in other kids in the family and neighbor kids. My mother worked in Head Start and in public schools; she worked in a couple of different schools. She would see kids who needed help and love, and she would bring them into our home. Mom and Dad would be their mom and dad, nurture them, and take care of them.

Now that I am an adult who has kids and grandkids, I'm amazed at what our parents did. It's a wonder to me that they had the ability to keep us so pure and so innocent in the midst of "Egypt." We lived in the midst of the roughest places, and yet, we had no clue about the world around us there.

I remember when my brother Darrell and I were teenagers, Mom would not only take care of the kids during the day, but she would babysit at night. We understood that she was helping the mothers who were waitresses at a local restaurant. There were all these kids at our house who sometimes stayed overnight. We lived in a small house, and there were already a lot of us living in that house.

When all these extra little kids were with us, we would often ask her, "Mom, why do you have all these kids? They were here all day long, are they going to go home at some point?" She would explain by saying, "Oh, their mom has to work late tonight, so she can't come." It wasn't until we were adults that we realized their moms were prostitutes in the evening. Mom was protecting those kids. If Mom and Dad didn't keep them, the mothers would take them along with them to their job. We had no idea what they did until years later.

Those kids are grown-ups now, and some come back and tell my parents, "Thank you, thank you so much!" They remember what our parents did for them and express their gratefulness. So do the ones they took care of in the daycare. As grown-ups, when we asked our mom about why they took care of all those children, she explained to us that the women were prostitutes. But that didn't matter to her. She just said, "We take care of people." It didn't matter to them what race, age, or issues they had. My parents believed that we need to take care of people. My parents took in kids that had severe trauma, every kind of trauma, so we had every kind of personality coming and going in our home for years.

One of the things Mom said when I was getting married to Troy was, "You choose who you love. You choose to love. When you choose to love, love changes everything." So, I have always chosen to love. Both of my parents were really good demonstrators. They weren't just preachers of the Gospel—they were demonstrators of the Gospel.

All my siblings are the same way, and they have married people who are happy that way. They look at people without judgment and ask, "How can we help them, how can we make a difference?" All of our walks look different, but we do the same thing. Our kids do the same thing. Our kids have been all around the world helping others.

People ask me all the time if it bothered me or if I was jealous of all those other kids. And the answer is no, we were never jealous; none of us were. For one, it was what we knew; we grew up in it, so we didn't know anything different. And two, there was no need to be jealous because we had just as much of our parent's time as they did, and we had as much as we wanted. We never went without. It is a miracle to me that we never went without. I don't know how my parents did it other than God is good to them. There was never any jealousy. We were taught very young to share and to be gracious to people. It has definitely helped in the walk I have now. You know there is nothing in God's Kingdom that goes to waste. Darrell and I talk about it a lot. Growing up in the areas where we grew up made us open to serving God in any place.

Up until I got married, we lived in places where we were the minority. We were usually the only white people wherever we lived, but we didn't know any difference. It made no difference to us, but it has helped me as an adult to be able to travel all around the world and feel comfortable, at home. Growing up in my house, there was every kind of nationality represented, and they were all my family. I have never had a thought about racism. I still don't understand racial prejudice because it makes no sense to me at all. I am grateful I don't comprehend it. The Lord placed me where He did on purpose so I could go to every nation and preach the Gospel and love people no matter what they look like. Cultures are different. But people aren't; we are all just people.

I went to public school and to public high school. I lived in a rough area and was in the minority. It's a crazy thing, but the Lord protected me during all of that. After I graduated from high school,

I attended beauty school. I remember coming home after the first week and telling my mom, "Mom, you are never going to believe this! Did you know girls smoke? And did you know they say bad words?" I remember the look on her face when she said, "Yes, I did know that."

I didn't grow up around that type of behavior. Even in public school and in the rough areas where we lived, people respected the anointing that my parents had so much that they didn't talk like that or act like that around me. It wasn't part of my life. I never saw it. It was like God had completely hidden all of that from me. The same was true for my siblings. We were hidden from all of that around us.

Being all that you can be isn't enough. I want you to be all that I am.

I look back on my life and see that God did that on purpose—just like it says in the Bible. God knew me even before I was formed (Jeremiah 1:5). He had a plan. This morning, I said to God, "Lord, I want to be all that You created me to be. I want to do that and be that."

He said, "No, that is not enough."

I responded, "What do You mean, Lord?"

"Being all that *you* can be isn't enough. I want you to be all that *I am*."

I realize that I am still learning at this age. It's not about everything I can give Him; it's about everything He can do through me.

I said, "Okay, Lord, I surrender to that."

I have seen incredible miracles including physical healings, spiritual healings, emotional healings, and financial healings. I have seen it all. I have seen it all and experienced it on a daily basis.

The most incredible miracle I have ever seen is a surrendered heart to God the Father. It is incredible to see people who truly surrender to Him in a way that makes them physically look different. A personal encounter with the Savior is the only way you will change. People can tell you whatever they want, but their experience is their experience. You have to have your own experience, and it has to be real. He is real. I have seen it, and I have experienced it daily.

2

Teachings on Raising Children

One of the things Troy would tell me from very early on was, "Don't protect our kids from Jesus." That was also demonstrated to me as a child. Our parents didn't protect us from whatever it was the Lord had called us to do. They didn't say you can't go there or go here. They would say, "Let God speak to you. Whatever He says, you can trust Him."

The safest place you can be is in the will of God. It doesn't matter where you live, it doesn't matter what you have, it doesn't matter who you know—the safest place to be is in His will. It was the greatest gift given to me. It is important to focus on knowing the will of God. Don't focus on things that aren't of Him. If you are saying, "That's the devil's music, that's the devil's this, or that's the devil's that," you have the wrong focus. What you look at is where you are going.

Troy and I got our motorcycle licenses a few years ago. I hadn't ridden since I was a kid, so I decided to take a refresher course. The guy teaching said, "Wherever you look is where you are going to go." He was demonstrating that, and I thought, *That's brilliant. That's a Kingdom principle.*

So if you are constantly telling your kids the devil is over there, they start looking for the devil in everything. They are going to find the devil. Don't point people to the devil. Point them to Jesus.

Jesus says that if you lift Him up He will draw all peoples to Himself (see John 12:32 NKJV). He didn't say if you tell them about the devil, they will be saved. No, that is not what He said. He said that if you lift Him up, they will be saved. So, it is really important to point your kids to Jesus. It's important that you are looking for Jesus in everything. I'm never looking for the devil. I'm telling you, the devil is looking out for me—to do me harm! (See 1 Peter 5:8.)

Wherever you look is where you are going to go.

One important lesson the Lord taught me a long time ago is that we are not to worry about our enemies. Let them flee from you. Let your enemies be afraid of you. Don't you be afraid of them. That was a big life change in thinking for me that came at a critical time. We had gone through an experience, as many pastors and Christians do, of walking through a church split. It was gut-wrenching, and I told the Lord, "I don't want to walk in unforgiveness. Lord, help me understand."

God said, "If you can see those people and do not want to go in the other direction, then you have forgiven them." So I said okay. I dealt with the situation with what He told me as the base level. If I could see them in the store and not want to turn and run, then I knew I had truly forgiven them.

Then God took it further. He said, "I know you don't want people to be your enemy. You know, though, there are people who make themselves your enemy. Some will stomp their foot on the ground and say, 'I'm making it my place to destroy you or to harm you, or whatever it is.' Don't worry about those people. Don't spend your time looking, listening, and paying attention to them."

In effect, God was telling me to say to them, "I don't give you the place in my life that deserves my attention. I'm not paying attention to *those things* because I am paying attention to who created me and told me who I am. He is the One telling me what I'm supposed to do. If I'm paying attention to you, then I'm not paying attention to Him."

I'm teaching this same thing to my kids and to my grandkids. My oldest grandson was going through a rough time with his self-esteem, which we all do. We learn while going through that phase. You have to learn not to coddle people through that. Let them learn what God is speaking to them. My grandson kept saying, "I'm not very smart. I'm stupid," and other comments like that. It went on and on.

So I said, "Are you created in God's image?"

And he said, "Yes."

"So you think God is stupid, and you think God isn't very smart?" I asked.

And he said, "Well, no, God is smart. He knows everything."

I said, "But you are created in His image."

"Well, yes," he replied.

"Then how can you be stupid and all those other things you're saying about yourself? Are you saying it because of the lies you are listening to? Stop listening to the lies and listen to the One who made you," I said.

That was a good life lesson. Not just for my grandson but for me, too. Most of the lessons I have learned are from being a mom and learning from my children or else from learning from the experiences of the kids who grew up with me. The Lord really speaks to me through the kids. Jesus says, *Let the little children come to Me...* (Matthew 19:14 NKJV). Because kids will believe you. And trust you. That's what He wants us to do. He wants us to believe Him and trust Him.

If you tell your grandkids that you are taking them to Disneyland, they are going to ask you every day, "Are we going to Disneyland today?" They will keep asking you because they believe you! We have to believe the Lord like that. Believe what He is saying and not listen to the enemy in the garden. That's where Eve got tripped up; she started listening to him and not to the Lord. What you focus on is where you are going.

3

Blended Family

Conforming ourselves to God's plan means being able to fit through the door that He opens for us. I love Lisa Harper and her Bible studies. She talks about her Spanx and says that if you were to cut them, she would pop like a can of biscuits. I thought that was so real. It prompted me to think about the fact that so many times, God presents us with open doors, and we are too big to walk through them.

Sometimes our ego or our baggage, our regrets, and our mindsets are too big to fit through that door. When that is the case, God tells us we have to get small, and we have to trust Him. You are going to have to be who He made you to be, not what someone else has labeled you to be, and not the expectations you have put on yourself. You can't be any of those.

Having a blended family was not something I ever thought I would have. I was 18 years old before I had a concept of people having a blended family. All the kids I grew up with had their parents. Whether it was the good, the bad, or the ugly, they had their parents, and that was their family. My parents were married until the day my dad passed away. That was just all I knew. I didn't know anyone who had stepparents. I didn't understand the concept. Looking back on it, I realize I knew people who did, but I just didn't know about that situation. I did go to public school, but I didn't know about that. I really did live a very sheltered life because God had a plan for me, and He kept me that way.

When I met Troy, he had a little girl. When we decided to get married, it meant that I was going to be a stepmom. The only thing I knew about stepmoms was from Disney movies. I grew up in California, so I knew Disney well. My thought was, *I don't want to be a wicked stepmother.* That was all I knew about them, and it was horrible.

I absolutely love our daughter. I loved her before she was my daughter. I remember talking to my mom about this. My mom probably thought, *What did I do? I must have dropped her on her head or something because this girl is broken.* But I came to her and said, "Mom, I'm really concerned that I'm not going to be as good of a mom to her as I should be because I am going to be a stepmom." My mom told me, "You choose who you love."

She reminded me of all the kids I grew up with and all the kids they had parented and continue to parent. When you look at all of us, you can't tell who was biological and who wasn't. We all grew up the same; they loved us all the same. People say that is impossible. It isn't. I have seen it, lived in it, and I grew up in it. When I looked at it like that, it really changed my perspective on what a blended family could be and should be.

I started praying about getting married and being a stepmom. My intention had been that I didn't want to get married until I was much older. I wanted to travel and do lots of things. I clearly heard the Lord speak and tell me that Troy was the one I was to marry. It was very loud and clear because marriage was not my intention at that time, and God wanted me to hear Him. I wasn't even going to date Troy; we were friends, we were prayer partners, and that was as far as I wanted to go with that because I had places I wanted to go and things I wanted to do.

Because God is long-suffering, patient, and caring, He took me through the process of putting on my Spanx and conforming my life to His image, not my own. I told the Lord that if I was going to get married, my intention was to have lots of kids. I did get married and I did have a little girl when I got married. I was told by other people that when I was married and we had our own kids, I was not going to love her the same. They said I would love mine more, and that it was okay to do that.

That truly rocked my world. It broke my heart. At first, I thought, *I just won't have any more kids because that's not fair to her. She didn't ask for this, and she doesn't deserve it. I love her, and I am not going to do that.* The Lord challenged me on that thought. The Lord said, "You are blended into My family, and I love you just as much as I do My other children." He reminded me of my parents and my upbringing and the truth of that experience. So Troy and I did have children; altogether, we have four.

Maegan is our oldest, and I can honestly say that I love her just as much as I love the other three. They are all my children. Maegan does have two families, but we are her family, and she is our family. She is the oldest, so she had her own room and her own things; and even though she wasn't there as much as the other kids, it was very much her home when she was with us.

The Lord said, "You are blended into my family. I love you as much as I do my other children."

Growing up in that role as a young mother, I met people my age who married people with other children, and I was shocked. I was heartbroken to see how other families did it. There was a mindset of "Those are your kids. These are my kids." I saw them treat the kids differently. It was mind-boggling to me to see how even Christian families felt this way. I knew I had to have a different mindset. God has called me to a different calling.

I also knew I had to speak up for these children who were in families like that. Even to people who were my friends, I learned to point out that they needed to recognize what they were doing. Treating kids differently is not Jesus. It is not fair to these kids, and it isn't going to work to build a healthy family. At a young age, the Lord made me an advocate for children in blended families.

It is okay to have blended families—family is still family. If you are going to marry someone who has children or has grandchildren, those kids become yours. If that is not okay with you, then don't get married. My advice to people who aren't able to love children like they are their own, and "do it as to the Lord," then do not get married. It is so selfish to think that you can go into a family and destroy it because you have a need that needs to be filled. I'm very outspoken about blended family situations.

OVERCOMING CHALLENGES

Blended families can work and can be the best for everyone. Are there challenges? Absolutely, but there are always challenges when you have children. There are challenges when you are married. There are challenges when you are single. There are challenges in life. You can't blame your challenges on the fact that you married someone who has a child who doesn't like you. No one can say their child loves them every moment of every day. When you are the disciplinarian, they don't always love you in that moment. Yet, you are the adult in the situation. You have been given the authority. God is going to hold you accountable for how you treat these children. If you are considering becoming part of a blended family, seek the Lord first.

Blended families have to balance the fact that there are two different families involved. The parenting will be different. You and your spouse parent differently because you grew up under different parenting styles. So did the other set of parents in your shared child's life. The shared child will grow up in two entirely different households and situations.

I have recently been talking to our daughter Maegan about her life. We all have to get to the place where we learn our own identity in Christ. As you mature, it is still a process. As our chapters change and bring different roles and different places, we still process with the Lord to understand who He wants us to be in the new things.

As I talked with Maegan, I told her that it is very impressive to me that she has become the woman she is and that she has accomplished all the things she has. Growing up in a blended family means you have one set of rules and expectations in one home, so you have to learn how to conform to that image. Then you go to the other home, and we all loved Jesus, which we all really do, but still, the homes were different because we were very different people. Even the sibling demographics in each home were different.

How is it that she has learned her identity so well since she had to be different in different places? She had to live with different expectations, different rules, and different ways the family functioned. We want our children to be able to be themselves, but it is hard for the children to figure that out when there are so many differences. We have to have grace for the children who are living in the middle of all this. We must have the awareness that even as an adult, this would be hard. How much harder it is for children to navigate this type of lifestyle while they are growing up?

The best case, the dream case scenario, is that both sets of parents learn to work together. That is one thing that our oldest daughter always had. We get along really well with her mom and her stepdad. They are wonderful people who love Jesus as well. We work together.

I have known many families where that is not the case. That is not how it works for them. In situations like that, think about Spanx. God's Word tells us to do all that we can to live in peace with everyone (Romans 12:18). That is extremely important in blended families. We must invite God to search our hearts to reveal any offense we are holding, resentment we have toward the other parents, or judgment against them we are holding on to. None of that is going to bring peace into situations. Any of those things can cause hurt in the child's heart.

Criticizing a child's parent is not what Jesus would have us do. He wants us to bring these difficult situations with us into prayer so He can purify our hearts and minds. There are things that will keep us from going through the door that leads to a joyful family, which He opened for us to walk through. Submitting to the Lord, asking Him to *create in us a clean heart*, and committing our will to do His will is an act of love. By this, we show we love the Lord and the precious children He has entrusted to our care.

ACTS OF LOVE

In those cases, it is also critical that you trust the Lord. You have to trust the Lord with your kids. That is the hardest thing the Lord has asked of me. I can lay down my life all day, every day, with no problem. I can go to the farthest corners of the earth and do whatever He asked me to. I could give away everything I have if He asked me. Yet when He said, "Do you trust Me with your kids?" that was gut-wrenching. There is more about this in the next chapter. The Lord will help each of us learn to trust Him with our children.

If you are in a blended family and it has gone wrong, go back and repent. Repentance is the greatest gift that God has given us. So many of us look at it as if it is a punishment, but it isn't a punishment. Repentance is God's way of trading something bad in our lives for something good that He has for us. He is saying, I have something so good for you if you will just say, "Look, God, I need Your help in this."

Troy and I grew up very differently. Our parenting styles were very different. There were times when he would say or do something that wasn't okay with me. I would tell him, "I know that seems normal to you, but it's not normal for me." We would then discuss it. If he agreed with me that maybe he should not have handled it like that or said what he did, he would always repent. He would even come before the kids and say, "Look, I said this, but this is what I meant, and I'm sorry." It is one of the things we did as a family that Troy is very, very good about, even to this day.

I would do the same thing. If I did something that wasn't right, I would go to the kids and admit that I was wrong. Doing that with our kids teaches them and shows them how to be emotionally stable. When they see their parents admit when they are wrong and repent, they learn. Kids listen to what we say, but they learn more from what we do than just what we say. The two must line up. Our actions will always speak louder than our words. If you say one thing and do something else, you send mixed messages to your kids. You are going to have mixed-up kids if you do that.

If you say that you go to church and you love Jesus, but you don't love your kids because they are "someone else's kids" and you can't deal with their other set of parents, then you are sending mixed messages. That's when you have a mess on your hands and want to blame someone else. If we look inward and talk to God about the mistakes we have made, He will meet us there. He wants to give you beauty for the ashes you have made. Nothing in the Kingdom goes to waste. He can help you turn the ashes into incredible learning situations. You can make it better by coming to Him with all your challenges.

Repentance is a place where God says, "Bring Me your dirty clothes, and let's wash those together. Let's get all the stains out of this. Let's get you a new garment." I love how gracious and kind He is. I'm so grateful that I grew up in the family I did. I'm especially thankful that my parents were very good at teaching us about the fear of the Lord. They taught us to respect the Lord.

In 1 John, chapter 4, verses 20-21 (NKJV) we find, *"If someone says, 'I love God,' and hates his brother, he is a liar; for he who does not love his brother whom he has seen, how can he love God whom he has not seen? And this commandment we have from Him: that he who loves God must love his brother also."* One of the reasons God's Word says that is because it is easier to love someone you can see than it is to love someone you can't see. So if you can't respect the people you can see, then how can you respect God, whom you can't see?

We must take that truth into our lives and understand that what we are doing outwardly in the natural world is what we are doing spiritually. Ask yourself these kinds of questions: "Do I have respect for the authority around me? Do I respect the schoolteacher, or do I assume that my child is always right?"

I have seen so many people really mess up their children with the position that the child is always right. They are not always right. It doesn't mean that every teacher is always right. What we must see, however, is that there is an authority above them, and we must teach our children to respect that authority.

When they learn to respect the authority around them in the natural, they will be able to respect God and His authority. If there is a problem with a teacher, you go take on that battle as an adult. You don't involve your child in that interaction or discussion.

Our children are very precious gifts God has given us, and we must have the emotional intelligence and enough common sense to recognize when children need to be involved and when they don't need to be involved.

For example, my parents never argued in front of us. Some think that is a good thing; others think it is bad. I am on the side that it is a good thing. I didn't know what was going on behind their closed doors. They didn't discuss their adult things with the children. We just knew that when they came out, they were unified. I don't even know if there were arguments or not. I do know there were times they would go behind closed doors and they would come out unified. They never allowed us to pit them against each other. So many times, people let their children in on conversations that are not for them.

We, as parents, must protect our children. God is holding us accountable for the precious gifts He has given us. They are only your children for a short time; then they become the parents, then the grandparents. We can see the trickle-down effect in our society now of the fact that our children have lost respect for authority. If we are going to break and change that cycle, it starts with us. We must respect God and respect authority. We can't look to other people to be the change; we have to be the ones to take responsibility.

We can't use excuses for not parenting well. We can't say that we don't know any better because our parents didn't parent us well. There is this amazing book titled the *Bible*, and it tells us better. Both of my parents came from very, very hard situations. If you knew their story, you would wonder how those two people parented any children, let alone hundreds of children. Particularly when you see how well all their children have turned out. It is a testimony of Jesus, and it is a testimony that the Bible works! When we eventually stand before Jesus, we will all stand there without excuse.

RESPECT

Respect starts in the home. Children must see parents respecting each other, and parents respecting their children and teaching them to respect their parents. In general, having children in a blended family or not, is one of the greatest gifts that God gives us. It is proof that He trusts us when He entrusts His kids to us so that we can raise them up in a way that honors and glorifies Him. We have to have the fear of the Lord to be able to do that. If not, we will raise them up in any way we choose based on emotions or what we value at the time. Our mindset must be that there is Someone higher than us that we are going to answer to someday.

We grew up helping with the work that had to be done in the house. We understood that some jobs were boys' jobs and some were girls' jobs. That is just the way it was, and I still do that to this day with my grandchildren. Boys are boys and girls are girls, and that will forever be a truth.

The boys would work outside on the weekends, and the girls would work inside. The girls would clean, cook, wash dishes, and do those kinds of jobs. My mom was really good at instructing us about what we were supposed to do. If we didn't want to clean the house or whatever she had asked us to do, she would say, "If you knew Jesus was coming to your house today, would you clean it?"

Our response was, "Of course we would!"

Then she would say, "He's here!"

She instilled in us that He is always here. We were taught to keep things clean because He is always here. Anytime we said something that was not a good thing to say, she would ask us a similar question, "Would you say that if you thought Jesus was sitting right there?" This caused us to think about that. Then she would reinforce that He is always right here.

We aren't to live our lives in the fear that Jesus is going to smack us or belittle us. We live knowing that He sees us. We are called to live our lives in the reverence and holiness that comes from know-ing He is here in our lives. When we live like that, then when we go through our times of trouble, we will *know* that He sees us.

When we say, "Lord, I need You," we don't doubt or question that He is there for us. Being able to instill that in our children and our children's children is such a privilege. For them to share our lives when we *know* He is with us gives them the experience of knowing it, too. That way, it isn't a theory—they *know* He's with them.

Having the mindset that knows He is here doesn't mean we won't do things we ought not to do. We all do those things. The Bible says all have sinned and come short of His glory (Romans 3:23). I know I have had my messes. I have made some knowingly and willingly sometimes. I think to myself, *I'm going to just go ahead and do this.* And the Lord is watching all this. He is aware it is a train wreck and that He will need to help me clean up the pieces afterward. He does, and He doesn't stand there with a pointed finger saying, "I told you so!" or "You shouldn't have done that."

He does talk to me about it, though. He might say, "Are you going to learn from this lesson, or are you going to go around this one again?" He is just so patient. I don't think people really understand that, so they can't teach it to their children. They need to know He is patient and He is kind, but He is also an authority figure. If there is a situation when it warrants a spanking, then you will get a spanking.

His Word tells us He chastens those He loves (Job 5:17; Hebrews 12:6; Revelation 3:19). If there is a time you need to be disciplined, He will discipline you. It isn't that He is mean or He is angry. It is for your benefit. He is telling us that if we don't stop those things, they will kill us and destroy our lives or someone else's lives. He will stop us.

It is important to have the fear of the Lord (Proverbs 1:7; Acts 9:31, Acts 19:17) and the respect that brings. We need respect for Him, for His house, for His holiness. We in the church, the body of Christ, have gotten away from respectfully fearing the Lord. That is on us. We can't wait for someone else, expect someone else, or hope someone else will return to that mindset. That's for us to do—daily.

4

Trust

I remember when the Lord asked me a very hard question about trusting Him. This was a time when we were going through a very hard situation, it was about 10 years into ministry. We had been doing well. We started off with really good long-time friends, good things were happening in the ministry, our kids were growing up together, and life was great. And then all of a sudden, everything just kind of made a left turn. Our very good friends decided they wanted to do something different; which was fine, but ultimately there was a lot of collateral damage in the mistakes we all made at the time due to some immature decision making.

They decided to do one thing, and we decided to continue doing what we were doing, but it wasn't in a way that was healthy for the congregation. It was a very hard situation, which made it very hard for our children. It was also very hard for me personally because these were friends, and the betrayal and the hurt was a lot to handle. So I came to the conclusion that I just didn't need friends. I didn't need any more friends. I was done. I was tired.

I thought, I have a husband who loves me with all of his heart. I have children who love me. I have an incredible family, and that works for me. This friend thing just doesn't work for me.

So with that said, a couple of years went by, and I actually did have a friend who is a friend now. She was working with us in the ministry as our secretary. But she was also way more than that. She was our right hand. There were four of us who worked together— Troy, my good friend Paula, and my brother-in-law. We all worked together in the ministry, and it was amazing. Things were getting better. It was hard work, but we overcame so many challenges. But for me personally, I was still really struggling with trusting people.

I remember Paula coming up to me one day as we were cleaning the church. We did everything together. She said, "Do you know what I want?"

I said I had no idea and asked, "What do you want?"

She said, "I just want you to be my friend."

At that moment, my heart broke. I thought, *Well, I thought we were friends.* And I remember telling her that she is a friend.

But she said, "No, you don't let anybody be your friend."

And I thought, *Wow. She just called me to the carpet on this.*

So I did a big heart evaluation on myself and asked, "Lord, is that true?"

And the Lord said, "Yes, it's very true. You have walls up and you don't let anybody in because you don't trust them."

"Wow, Lord, that won't work in ministry." I told the Lord that He was going to have to really help me navigate through this time and teach me because I was lost, again.

I'm open about the fact that I get lost. And I got lost at this time, and I had been lost and didn't even realize I was lost. That's how lost I was. And I remember praying about it and seeking the Lord about it and talking to Paula about it. She really was my friend. I just was not a very good friend at the time because I was so hurt and so broken and didn't even realize it.

And so, as I'm navigating through this with the Holy Spirit, I remember praying to the Lord one night. I was talking to Him, pouring my heart out to Him, and asking, "Lord, what's wrong with me? Why am I like this?"

The Lord spoke to me, saying, "Leana, do you love Me?"

My answer was, of course, "I love You, Lord. I love You."

I was thinking, *I know when You asked Peter this what was going on, but I don't know what's going on with me that You're asking me this. Am I going to do something wrong? Am I going to betray You or something crazy?*

And He just asked me again, "But do you love Me?"

And I said, "Lord, I love You with all my heart. I do everything I do for You and because of You. Otherwise, I wouldn't do any of this." And so the third time I'm expecting the same question because that's what had happened to Peter, but it wasn't the third time.

He said, "But do you trust Me?"

And I pondered it for a minute, and said, "Well, of course I trust You. I go all the way to Africa. I go to Mexico, I go to all these places and I give You my life. If I were told to go tomorrow, Lord, I trust You in that."

And then He said, "But do you trust Me with your kids?"

Wow, that was right between the eyes. My first thought, *Are You kidding me?* I knew the answer as soon as He asked me. It's not like anyone can lie to Him. And I said, "Lord, no. No, I don't. I don't trust anybody with my kids."

And the Lord said, "You can't really love Me if you don't trust Me. You have to trust Me."

The Lord said, "You can't really love Me if you don't trust Me. Trusting is a part of loving."

Trusting is part of loving. That was a hard one. That was really, really hard. That was harder than Paula asking me if I would be her friend. Wow, that one took my breath away.

I sat there not knowing how to respond to that or even what to say and just crying and saying, "God, I don't know how to fix this. I don't know how to change this. I don't know what to say about this." And I repented, and I said, "Lord, I want to trust You with my kids. I really do, but I love my kids more than I love anybody or anything next to my husband. I don't know how to trust You with my kids."

Then the Lord started walking me through it because He's so gracious and He's so kind. He said, "You have to trust Me with your kids. I love your kids more than you love your kids. I love your kids so much that I let them be part of your life. I trust you. I trust that you're going to take care of your children, My children. Just as I asked Mary to take care of My only begotten Son, I'm asking you to take care of these children. They're actually My children."

And what a reality shock that was for me. Now, all of a sudden, I was not just taking care of my kids but understanding these are God's kids, and He is trusting me to take care of them. I wasn't just physically taking care of them, but spiritually, emotionally, and financially, and in all areas of their lives.

I had to ask the Holy Spirit to help me navigate what that meant. How do I be a parent to the Lord's kids? How do I do this? How do I partner with Him? *How do I partner with You, Holy Spirit?* And I realized I had taken so much control over my kids' lives that I wasn't giving the Lord any room to have His way with them. So I had to trust Him and say, "Okay, God, I'm trusting You that whatever they go through, You're there with them and with me."

And I still very much, even to this day when they're all in their 30s. I have to allow them to navigate with the Lord in their own walk. Because their walk is their walk.

This encounter with the Lord happened when they were all very small children. The Lord has been so faithful to my kids. All four of my kids and their spouses love the Lord with all of their hearts. All of my grandkids love the Lord with all of their hearts. And I have seen miraculous and amazing happenings through my kids' lives. In the times they were going through something painful, I would think, *Oh, I could have saved them from that.* But then I could hear the Lord telling me, "Leave them alone. I've got this." Then I could stand back and go, *Okay, God, I trust You in this.*

I deliberately allowed Him to show me and tell me what I needed to know. He would tell me that my kids were not going to learn if I didn't let them go through some challenges.

We can't protect our children from Jesus. I didn't even realize that I was doing that until that time. What a lesson that was for me.

So when we focus on not being lost, a lot of times we realize we are holding on to things that really don't belong to us.

You have to trust the Holy Spirit. The Holy Spirit isn't a spooky spiritual thing that gives you the heebie-jeebies. The Holy Spirit will not make you do crazy things or say crazy things. The Holy Spirit is a real Person, and He leads us and guides us. He is what some people call their conscience. But He is much more than that. He is part of the Godhead, the Trinity: God the Father, God the Son, God the Holy Spirit (Matthew 28:19). He is that feeling inside you. He is that right mind. He is the goodness, the kindness that instructs us and teaches us (John 14:26; Luke 3:22).

If your kids are going to learn, you have to let them go to school, or you have to school them. But they still have to learn arithmetic. They have to learn reading. They have to learn writing and all of the basic skills. And so many times, as our children are growing up, we want to protect them from all of those skills. But if they don't learn how to have social skills on top of all of those things, it doesn't do them any good. Because if you don't have social skills, you can't make it out in the world. And it's the same way in the Kingdom. Your kids have to have Kingdom skills. And if they're going to learn how to walk, they're going to fall a couple of times, and they're going to get up, and they're going to be fine.

It's going to hurt for a second, but they're going to be fine. They're going to learn how to walk. They're going to learn how to be independent. They're going to learn how to be strong. They're going to learn for themselves how to hear the Holy Spirit speak. I had to learn all of that as a young parent. I learned by asking the Lord to help me through. And now I'm learning it as a grandparent.

Now I have grandkids, and because I know what Jesus did with my kids, I can trust Him with my grandkids. Being able to trust the Lord in every step that I make has been a beautiful part of my journey. And I don't just see it in my own kids' lives, I see it all around the world with the kids that the Lord brings to us.

THIS IS THE ONE

God will take us into a situation, and we think we're done for the day. Then all of a sudden, He highlights this one kid and says, "This is the one. This is the one I want you to go after, that one right there."

That happened a little over a year ago in the Amazon region of Brazil while we were ministering also in Columbia, Brazil, and Peru. We were at a children's outreach across the border from where we were staying. I was there with a really good friend of mine, Anna Barber, and, of course, my husband. We had a team of people with us at a kid's crusade. At the end of the crusade we were asked to lay hands on each one of the kids. So, of course, I said I would.

I was at the front of the line with the pastor and his wife, and we were laying hands on every kid who came to us. These kids speak Portuguese. I can speak some Spanish, but I don't speak any Portuguese. So, I had no idea what the kids were saying and they had no idea what I was saying. But the Holy Spirit, again, makes sense of circumstances when there seems to be no way. Consequently, the time was beautiful, an incredible time of connecting and praying with the children. I don't know how many went through the line, at least a hundred kids. My friend Anna came up to me and said, "Leanna, I need you to come over here. I need you to come. I need you to talk to this little girl."

I went with her and met a sweet little girl, a 13-year-old named Mayelli. She was beautiful, so precious. When I looked at her, I knew instantly that she had been being prostituted. And it broke my heart. It made me so sad. At first I didn't say anything to her. I just looked at her. I looked at the shoes and clothes she was wearing, and I knew she had just come off the street. I could see that life that was in her beautiful little face.

I definitely have a shoe thing. I love, love, love shoes. I have a huge fondness for shoes. I have some shoes that are special to me. It's not that they're expensive, it's not that they're designer or any of those things. They're special to me because of where I bought them or the situation I was in when I got them. Memories are attached to the shoes, so each pair means something different.

When I was packing to go on this trip to Brazil, I needed some water sandals, so I packed a pair of flip-flops that I take everywhere with me. That's what I had in my suitcase to wear for the morning. I got up, looked in my suitcase, and that's not what I found. I found another pair that I call my "Jerusalem shoes." When I found those sandals, I wondered why they were there. I usually don't take them anywhere. I don't travel with them. I had bought these particular shoes at the Jordan River when I was going to baptize several friends and family members. I wore those in the Jordan River as I was baptizing, so they are my special Jerusalem shoes. I know Jerusalem is not near the Jordan River, but that's what I call them. So I don't travel with them because they are important to me. They're special to me.

That particular morning, when they were the only shoes I could find, I couldn't imagine why I had brought them. But I put them on and off I went to the kids' crusade. When Anna introduced me to sweet young Mayelli, I looked at what she was wearing. Her shoes were high heel stilettos and she was wearing very skimpy little clothes. I said, "Mayelli, you have to take off those shoes." She took them off, and she was barefooted. She said, "I don't want to wear these anymore. I don't want to wear these anymore."

I told her she didn't have to wear them anymore. Then she looked at me and said, "Will you please be my mama?"

Oh my, that made me cry. "Yes, of course I will. I will be your mama." I asked her if I could pray for her. I prayed for her and led her to the Lord. In that moment, the Lord told me, "I want you to take your shoes off your feet and give them to her because she's going to have a different walk. Your shoes represent your walk."

I said, "Yes, Lord, I will." Then I looked down and saw my Jerusalem shoes. I thought, *Wow, Lord, You knew what I was going to be doing with these. I didn't know, but of course You did.* And I gave her my shoes.

A NEW WALK

It wasn't just that I gave her my shoes—they were special shoes that meant something to me. And the Lord was telling me in that moment that her walk is changing forever. And I was so grateful that my friend Anna had the heart and the ability to hear the Holy Spirit speak and say, "This is the one." Anna had been ministering to her and had been loving her, and she brought her to me and the Holy Spirit did the rest. We brought Mayelli into our family. This sweet, sweet, beautiful little girl found out just a couple of months later that she was pregnant. She had been pregnant when she came there that night but didn't know it. And now we have a beautiful grandson from Mayelli.

Through my husband's ministry, Troy Brewer Ministries, we were able to rescue Mayelli from the sex trafficking atrocity that had held her captive. We placed her in a secure place and took care of her and her beautiful little boy. We gave them hope for a better future. We're her family. She still calls me Mom and calls Troy, Papa Troy and loves us—and we will always love her.

What I want to tell you about Mayelli is that she's a rescuer now. Her walk changed from having to be a prostitute at a very young age. God transformed her whole walk through the rest of her life. She knows where other young girls and boys are who are in this demeaning lifestyle—not by their choice, not by their doing. Mayelli now goes out and tells the ones who want out that there is hope, there is another way of life. She brings them to us, telling these youngsters that we are the people who will help them. She says, "My family will help you."

That is the most beautiful reward we could ever ask or hope for. Money is just money. I always tell anyone who asks me, "Money is just zeros, a means to an end. There's no power in money. There's no life in money. The only thing money is good for is to do the work that we want to do all around the world. And we get to do that. The Holy Spirit leads us and guides us into amazing places. The Holy Spirit gives to us. What He gives us, we allow to flow through us, because He freely gives, and we freely give." We have testimonies like Mayelli's. We have thousands of those type of life-changing testimonies from kids who were rescued. Each is a beautiful reward that we cherish.

Our own four children are all in a ministry of helping people, of changing people's lives. And now I see the devotion and commitment to other people in my grandchildren. My oldest grandson is only 11 now, but I see him doing ministry, and I see the transformation in his life. That only comes from allowing the Lord to navigate for you, letting the Holy Spirit take you and lead you and guide you. And listening when He says, "Okay, you're lost in this one area, but I'm going to help you find your way."

You may be lost in relationships. You may be lost in addiction. You may be lost about who you are, your own identity. You may be lost in whatever thought process you've always relied on. But the Lord says you don't have to be lost—He found you. The Bible says in John 8:32 (NKJV), *"And you shall know the truth and the truth shall make you free."* Truth is found where the Holy Spirit is leading you and guiding you. You can trust Him. You can trust Him with all of your heart. You can trust Him with everything you are. He's not going to leave you or forsake you (Hebrews 13:5). He's not going to lead you in the wrong way. He's always going to lead you to the truth. He's always going to lead you into life. And there's always life more abundantly (John 10:10).

You might go through stuff in life, but you never go through it alone. And you will always come out the other side. When you do, you're going to say, "Wow, what I learned through that was so valuable to me that I would not have missed going through that for anything." What we go through in our life means something. There is a reason, a point, a purpose to it all. We should be able to look back on it and say, "What the devil meant for evil, the Lord meant for beauty. He gave me beauty for ashes, and I would do it again and again if I knew this was going to be the outcome." That's how you know when you're being led by the Holy Spirit—when it's beautiful.

SECTION TWO

Lord, Who Do You Say I Am?

We have become His poetry,

a re-created people that will fulfill

the destiny He has given each of us,

for we are joined to Jesus,

the Anointed One.

Even before we were born,

God planned in advance

our destiny and the good works

we would do to fulfill it!

Ephesians 2:10 TPT

5

On the second trip Troy and I made to Uganda, the Lord told me He had a ministry for me. At the time, I didn't know how I could do anything else. My ministry was to my husband and kids, and that was a lot. I was busy full time with everything we had going on. We had four kids, and there were two teenagers who were living with us at the time. We were busy at church and ministry, and Troy was also working at the time. It was a lot. Yet, I had clearly heard the Lord.

Hearing this from Him was surprising, because I had been very clear with Him from the beginning. I had resisted the idea of Troy being a pastor, but once God made it clear Troy had an anointing to carry out God's plan, I surrendered my opinion. When Troy accepted his calling, I pledged to fully devote myself to the ministry of taking care of him, our children, and the household. I was very happy with that role.

God is so good, and His plan is perfect for us. I love children and always have compassion for widows. So when He told me He wanted me to take care of orphans and widows, I gave Him my yes. Next, however, I did ask Him for confirmation that I had heard correctly.

Some of the villages we go into are unimaginably poor, particularly through the eyes of those of us who live in the affluent areas of the world. Try to visualize living in a mud hut with no food available to you and your family. Most people are barely surviving on what they can scrape together to eat. Now, think about how you would feel if you were in one of those villages as a missionary, and the people there were so grateful that you had come to serve among them that they offered you whatever small amount of anything they had.

While serving these kind people they have brought us two eggs, someone else brought us a small serving of beans, and we also were offered a chicken. These are heart-breaking moments for me. The last thing I want to do is take something from them. Yet, we know we would insult them if we don't accept their gift.

I asked the Lord to confirm what He said about the ministry He had for me by letting me go through this trip without having to take anything from any of the people.

When we arrived at our destination in Uganda, we connected with our friend who served as a pastor there. He is a joy to know. He lives in a hut and ministers at a tiny shack that serves as the church. What he lacks in resources is more than made up for by his great love for Jesus. As always, he enthusiastically greeted Troy. But then, with great excitement, he came directly to me, saying, "Come, I want you to meet someone."

Leading the way, he began telling me about the man he wanted me to meet. This man lived in the bush for over 40 years as a madman. He would throw himself into fires, have convulsions, and exhibit other demonic behavior. The tone of the pastor's voice shifted from excitement and held quite a bit of wonder in it as he told me that the Lord had sent him into the bush to save the man. "He has been staying with me ever since. He is glad you have come."

A few short steps later, a small man who looked like someone who had just come from a long time spent in the bush came walking toward me. His only possession was a filthy, ragged loin cloth which he wore. His face, however, was covered with a beautiful, radiant smile common to all who have had a profound encounter with Jesus. His hand, tightly clutching something small, was thrust toward me. Through interpretation, he said, "I knew you were coming, so I saved this to give to you."

He dropped a tiny coin with a monetary value of one-half penny into my outstretched palm. I didn't want to take it, but I knew it would insult him if I didn't.

I went back to the bus while the rest of the team was still ministering. I told the Lord that I didn't think that had been fair and talked to Him about how frustrated I was.

When Troy got on the bus, he could tell I was crying and asked me what was happening. I told him about the man and his gift and pointed him out to Troy.

Troy said, "Oh, Leanna, don't worry about that man. Holy Spirit prompted me to give him 20,000 shillings. He's going to be fine."

Within minutes, the rest of the team returned to the bus, and amazingly, all four of them told me the same thing. They each gave the man 20,000 shillings. The Lord taught me well that day. He explained that people needed to give so they could come to understand that He is a giving God. He saves us and redeems us so we can live with Him and join Him in Kingdom work. He loves to give to us, and as we grow in our relationship with Him, He will use us to give to others. He blesses us so we can be a blessing to others.

The Lord knew I felt unsure about my ability to have a ministry, and He used the encounter with the bushman that day to show me that I only needed Him to reach others. I realized that even if I were a billionaire, there was no way I could outgive our God.

The Lord recalled incidents from my childhood that helped me understand His hand had always been on my life. I was hit by a car when I was two and again when I was eight; I drowned two different times, and I had epilepsy during my childhood. Recalling all that helped convince my heart that He had set me apart "for such a time" as I was entering (Esther 4:14). It was a timely reminder that no weapon formed against us will stand when we are in God's hands (Isaiah 54:17).

The day after I met the bushman was a long day of ministry. We were in the mountains in Uganda. By the end of the day, we came to the bottom of a large hill. We spent the night in a small cinderblock house with no electricity. There was only a small candle that didn't have enough oxygen to give out much light.

He loves to give to us, and He will use us to give to others. He blesses us so we can be a blessing to others.

A DEMON AND A DREAM

I usually fall quickly asleep when my head touches my pillow at night. Just as I lay down, though, I noticed a purplish-blue light in the corner of the room. Troy saw it, too. Then, a horrible, demonic voice came from that corner. I was shocked by what it was saying. I had never heard such horrible things before. It was terribly disturbing, but I didn't feel any fear. I *know* with all assurance, that Jesus is the Author and Finisher of my faith, and He is always with me.

Troy had experienced this kind of encounter, so he immediately began to pray and rebuke the demon. I joined in, but it did not go away immediately. We then began to praise and worship King Jesus, and it left.

Troy went in to talk to the missionary, who was not surprised by his news. He even knew what it looked and sounded like and how it operated. "Oh, yes," he said, "that is the spirit that comes before the rebels come. We must pray." They prayed together for a while. I put my head on my pillow, thinking that I had had enough adventures for the day, and quickly went to sleep. The Lord, however, was not finished and gave me a powerful dream.

In the dream, God showed me the mission He had for me, including great details about it. He even gave me the name. It was definitely from Him because I would never have come up with it. The name is an acronym for what He gave me to do: SPARK Worldwide, which stands for Serve, Protect, and Raise Kids Worldwide.

The next morning, the missionary told us that the rebels had come within a few miles from where we were. They had killed many Ugandans in a nearby village, decapitated them, and laid their heads on the road. They had made many orphans out of precious children that night. We left and went to the west side of Uganda.

6

The Story of Colin

I t all began with one boy. We were at a big crusade in Fort Portal in the western region of Uganda. There were thousands of people in attendance, and Troy was about to go onto the stage to preach. He was in an area roped off from the people. It was terribly noisy, and security personnel were standing by the roped-off area. Nevertheless, a little boy managed to get through the crowd and the security, and he went right up to Troy and said, "Sir, you must feed me, for I am hungry," he said respectfully but loud enough to be heard over all the noise. He spoke proper British English because that is what they are taught in this part of the country.

Troy looked at him for a second and then said, "I must feed you because you are hungry?" The little boy quickly confirmed that was what he had said, "Yes! You must feed me."

Troy came back with a quick response. "Okay, well, stay with my wife while I speak, then we are going to go eat, and we will take you with us. Okay?" The boy nodded in agreement and turned and looked at me.

So here was this little boy who seemed to be around 8 or 9. He spoke English very well and was very proper and polite. His clothes were tattered, but clean. His shirt was buttoned up nicely. He looked healthy. I asked him what his name was, and he said, "Colin." I was a young mom, and I wasn't experienced out in the world yet. This was a big crowd, and this kid was by himself.

I said, "Where's your mom and dad?"

He said, "I don't have one."

Then I said, "Well, where are your grandparents?"

He said, "I don't have any."

I said, "Well, who do you live with?"

Once again, he answered, "I don't have any."

I thought maybe this was just a translation problem. I have an accent, and he has an accent, so at this point I wasn't sure what the problem was, but I could see we were not getting anywhere. So, I asked, "Well, where do you live?"

He said, "I will show you." I went with him, and even though I knew better than to walk off with people, I still did it.

He led me into a little alleyway between two buildings. One of the things they do in Uganda that I haven't seen anywhere else is sweep their dirt. I've seen it done in other places, but not to the extent that they do it here. They have the ability to sweep the dirt until it looks like concrete. It is amazing to see. His little place was meticulous, even though it was dirt. It was so clean. He had a couple of pieces of tattered clothing there. They were clean and folded properly. He had a couple of belongings.

He said, "I live here."

I remember just looking at him and said, "You live here?" He nodded. "But who do you live with?"

"I don't live with anybody, I have no one," he said, and this time I knew we didn't have a communication issue.

My reaction was, "Well, that's going to change." Then I thought, *Lord, this is an orphan. This is the ministry You called me to.*

We walked back to the crusade together and listened to Troy finish speaking. When he was done, I told him that he had to come to see where this little boy lived. I had tears in my eyes as I said, "I can't tell you. You have to see for yourself."

We went back to the alley and Troy was as astonished as I was. We had heard about orphans, and we had seen the commercials on TV. We had heard the stories; after all, we grew up in church and had seen pictures of situations like this.

But to actually see a child who lived by himself on the streets, particularly one who could be the same age as my child, was just overwhelming. We decided to take him to eat, and while there we would figure out what to do. So many people will pick up stray animals and have compassion for them, yet there are children living on the streets. They become such familiar sights that people just look past them. Heaven forbid we ever get that way!

We took Colin with us to meet several pastors from this big crusade to eat together. They saw us walking up with this little boy and began to shoo him away. We said, "No, he's with us. He isn't a random child following us. He is with us."

They said, "You can't bring him with you."

We said, "Yes, we can. He is with us. He is hungry, and we are going to feed him."

They said, "But you don't know him."

We explained that he was an orphan and that we had gone to where he lived. Feeling like they just didn't understand, we said, "He is all by himself, and there is nobody. It isn't like we are going to get into trouble for taking this little boy. He doesn't have parents, grandparents, or anybody. He is living on the streets." One pastor turned to us and said, "There are thousands of them."

"There are thousands of them." Troy replied, "I don't know thousands. But I know this one and he is no longer going to be an orphan."

Troy quickly replied, "I don't know thousands of them. But I know this one. This one is no longer going to be an orphan; he is ours, and he is going to dinner with us."

The pastors didn't appreciate this. Some of them understood, but some of them didn't. They didn't like us bringing along this little boy. Then Troy said, "I'm not doing any more work with you. I am now stopping everything I came here to do, and I am taking care of this little boy."

We took him with us, fed him, and got him a place to stay that night. The next day, we went to one of our partners there and said, "You have to help us. We don't know what to do. We don't know the customs or the culture here. We don't even know where to begin to get this little boy the help he needs."

Our friend said that most kids who don't have parents go to boarding school but have to pay fees. We told him we weren't familiar with boarding schools, so he took us to several of them. We found Colin one and put him in the boarding school so he would have a place to live and a place to be educated. He was smart, and he wanted to go to school, but he hadn't been able to go. We got him settled there, and he stayed at that boarding school for about a year.

We went back and checked on Colin and realized it wasn't a good situation. It was better than being homeless on the streets, but it wasn't a great boarding school, so we put him in a different one. He thrived there, and we continued to pay for him to go there. After a couple of years, we moved to the other side of the country to do work, but we continued to pay for his boarding school.

Because of Colin, we saw how boarding schools were run. We didn't want to criticize what the people there were doing because we knew they were doing the best they knew, but we wanted to do it the way God would have us to do it. Because of Colin, we started managing our schools the way we still do. All kids get to come, no matter if they have money or not. They are sponsored in one way or another. We also check on our schools and make sure they are being run the best way possible. We make sure the kids are being loved, that they are being protected, and that they are being nurtured. They are also being taught the Gospel and not just being taught *about* it; the Gospel is *demonstrated*.

So many kids have cycled through our systems and are now grown-ups who are doing the same thing. One young man named Jordan is in his late 20s. He went to school and became a humanitarian lawyer. His goal is to rescue and raise a thousand kids! I have other kids around his age who all grew up together in our first school. One has become a heart surgeon, another is a mechanic, and another is a pastor. They work collectively to reach out to save homeless kids. They also reach out to kids in schools to encourage them. When we get together, we ask them, "Why are you doing this? Why are you helping these kids?" They say, "Because this is what you taught us. It all started because of Colin."

7

Jimmy's Story

When the Lord brings people into our lives who have great and obvious needs, we may think meeting those needs is the reason Jesus connected us to them. So many times, however, as we meet those people's needs, our hearts and lives are changed by the lessons we learn. Jimmy was one of those people.

Jimmy was my precious little boy who I loved with all my heart. The lessons I learned from this little guy have definitely changed me forever. His life brought me a whole new perspective, a whole new love, and a whole insight into God's goodness. I met Jimmy on one of the trips to Uganda.

A group of four ladies and a young man who was an intern went to do children's crusades with Pastor David Musitwa. He decided to take us to the Rakai District, where AIDS had broken out many years ago. This district was ground zero for the epidemic. It is a long drive from where we were, and it is not safe to drive there at night. The roads are bad, but it's dangerous to drive at night in any third-world country. We drove out early in the morning to give us time to have the crusade all day and leave around three o'clock for the four-hour drive back.

We had the whole day planned out, and we had a super good day. We started off with an incredible church service, and then I had the privilege of performing my first marriage. I had no idea I was going to be ordaining a marriage that day, but I did, and it was fun. Pastor David came to me and said, "Mom, I want you to meet this man. He's a doctor from here in Uganda and works at the Mayo Clinic doing research on infectious diseases. He is studying AIDS and other infectious diseases that come from East Africa. He's here right now for about a month."

I said, "Okay, that's great, let's go meet him." We went to his little village house, and I met Dr. Noah, this very, very sweet man. I don't remember his last name. He was very gracious to greet us and to talk with us.

From there, we started the crusade at about 11 o'clock. Hundreds and hundreds of kids came to the crusade because when we have a crusade, we feed everybody in the village. That's a big, big deal when you don't know where your next meal is coming from. And they are definitely not going to miss the chance to eat what we have for them. They ate beef and had sodas and lots of food that are a big treats for the whole village. We also brought toys for the kids and did puppet shows. It was amazing, and the kids loved it. It was so great, so full of energy, and so full of hope.

My sister-in-law, Mendy Knight, was one of the ladies who went with me on this trip. While talking we noticed that we didn't see anyone around our age. Mendy is about six or seven years younger than me. We started talking to the pastors about this oddity and were told that almost all of our generation was gone. They died of AIDS because that is the generation that it hit hardest.

The parents of the kids who attended the crusade had died, so they were raised by elderly grandparents or by older siblings. There was a whole big gap of people who were missing, which I had never seen before or experienced before. It was interesting to be there, the landscape was very different from other parts of Eastern Uganda where there was a very diverse and beautiful landscape. The people are beautiful, too. The Spirit of the Lord is present there in an incredible way.

It was about 3 o'clock, and almost time to leave. Pastor David told me to get our team together because we needed to get on the road. He is very cautious and takes very good care of us. We were on the border of Tanzania and Uganda and wanted to make sure we would leave on time. He's a little overprotective, which I am grateful for; he has kept me and my team safe all these years. I'm a little bit of a rule-breaker. I try to stay where I'm supposed to stay, but I do kind of wander, so it is a full-time job for him to take care of me and the team.

I went and started rounding up my team, telling them we only had a little bit longer before we needed to start driving back. Everybody agreed, but I couldn't find Mendy. I couldn't find her anywhere. There were hundreds of kids and lots and lots of people. But we do stand out because we are the only *mzungu,* meaning white people. I was looking and looking, and finally I saw Mendy off in the distance. She was talking to a little boy. She came to me and said we needed to get this little boy some medicine. The little boy had the biggest smile I have ever seen on anybody's face.

THE 100 PERCENT ORPHAN

He was maybe nine or ten years old and was a true, 100 percent orphan. He lived by himself, on the ground, under a tree, and scavenged for food. He lived some hours away, so he had walked to the crusade. His chest, not just his stomach, protruded—both were big and very unusual looking. I had never seen anything like it in all my travels. Mendy asked me if I had any kind of medicine because his stomach was hurting him, and he was not doing well. She wanted us to get him some medicine before we left. I told her that I didn't think the kind of medicine that we had was going to fix him; it didn't look like a stomach issue to me. We've seen worms and all of those things, and I knew his problem wasn't that. I just didn't know what it was.

In that moment, the Lord reminded me of Dr. Noah. I thought, *You know, it's not a coincidence that we met him and the Lord opened that door, and there is favor there.* We took little Jimmy to Dr. Noah. It turned out that Dr. Noah had met Jimmy before, and since Jimmy doesn't speak any English, Dr. Noah told us about Jimmy. He said that this little boy lives a couple of hours away, and he lives by himself. He will come here occasionally and get help, but he just lives off of the ground. He said what's wrong with him is he's been eating cassava root. You can eat it if it is prepared properly. Otherwise, it can be poisonous and it causes water to get around your chest cavity. That causes heart failure, which is indeed what was going on with Jimmy.

Jimmy was talking to Dr. Noah, and he was translating for us. He told us that Jimmy heard the crusade was going to be here today, and he wanted to come. So he started walking very early in the morning to get here. It had taken him all day long because he couldn't walk very fast because he couldn't breathe. He told us it had taken him all day, and he was so sad that he missed it and that we were about to leave. He told Jimmy he was sorry he missed it. I told him he hadn't missed anything, we're still here, and everything we have, we're going to give to him.

Then I told him that we were not leaving until he was taken care of. I said, "You are a doctor; how can we fix him? What will it take to take care of this little boy?" He told us that he had fluid around his chest cavity, and they would have to go in with a really big needle and drain out all the fluid. Removing that fluid would help him breathe, but the doctor said that he was not that kind of a doctor. He said he had a local friend who could do that. He said he would call and see if he could come right now. I said I didn't care what the cost was, that it didn't matter to me. I told him I was not leaving there until this was taken care of.

So he called his doctor friend, and the doctor came over and did the procedure. There was no anesthetic, no nothing to ease the pain. They just stuck a huge needle in his chest and drained out the fluid. It was one of the most horrible things I've ever seen in my life. Jimmy just stood there and smiled the whole time. Dr. Noah told him that we were there to help him.

I told Dr. Noah and the other doctor that we wanted Jimmy's heart problem fixed permanently. The other doctor said there was a heart surgeon in Kampala that Jimmy could go to, and they would take care of him there.

"Okay," I said, "let's get him there today, not tomorrow, today." The challenge with that was that a patient has to have a caregiver with them in the hospital. Their hospital system is not like ours. A patient's caregiver gives the medicine, takes care of the bed sheets, and all of those things. So we found a widow in the village who was willing to do that. As we were getting her situated, getting Jimmy situated, and the hospital ready to receive him, Dr. Noah talked to Jimmy.

I CAME PRAYING

The whole time all this was going on, Jimmy just smiled. He loves, loves, loves Jesus. Dr. Noah said, "Jimmy, do you know that God sent these people from the West to take care of you?"

Jimmy smiled and said, "Yes, I know. I came praying."

In that moment, I thought, *If I had that kind of faith, if I had the kind of faith that Jimmy had, what could I do? What difference could I make? Jimmy* **believed.** "Yes, I know, I came praying," is on the walls of my clinics in Africa.

> ## Dr. Noah said, "Jimmy, do you know that God sent these people to take care of you?" Jimmy smiled and said, "Yes, I know. I came praying."

We took Jimmy to the hospital. The next day, I went to the hospital in Kampala to visit him. I talked to the heart surgeon and he could do the procedure, but Jimmy's heart was very far gone. He had been an orphan for too long and there was a lot of damage. I told him that I didn't care what it cost and he had to do the surgery, and so they did it. Before I left the hospital that day, I called my husband. Jimmy talked to Troy and said, "Daddy, I love you, and I thank you, and I know you are praying for me."

I was about to leave and said, "Jimmy, I'll be back tomorrow." He just looked at me, and said, "I want to go where you go." That broke my heart. I wanted to take him with me, but I couldn't because he had to be in the hospital for the surgery. The rest of my trip was not about all the things I had come to do—it was about Jimmy.

We took him coloring books and things we thought he'd like. I absolutely 10,000 percent hate hospitals. I hate them in the States; I hate them everywhere. Being in a hospital is just terrible for me. But I love Jimmy, so I was at the hospital every day making sure he was okay. My sister-in-law, Mendy, was with me, and we just loved on him and encouraged him. I told him that we were going to take him back to the United States. I said I was going to figure out a way to get him and bring him home with me.

When I returned home and talked to Troy about it, we knew we had to bring him home with us, and we had to take care of him. We knew this little boy literally had nobody. So we started the process. You can imagine what a long process this was. At the time, we had no resources, but we had Jesus, and we had a word. It was going to take a long time to get through the process, so I went back to visit Jimmy and talk to the surgeons.

Finally, they told me he had to have the surgery immediately. There were only two places that were able to do the heart surgery that he needed. They told us that we could take him to India or we could take him to Israel, either one. At the time, I didn't know anyone in Israel, but it didn't matter to me. I didn't really care which of the two. I just wanted him to have the best heart surgeon because they couldn't do the kind of surgery he needed there in Uganda.

I returned home, we got the surgery set up, and we made plans for him to go. We were working on the adoption and making plans to bring him here to be part of our family. Then I got a phone call, and they told me that Jimmy had died.

NEVER ALONE AGAIN

I remember talking to the Lord and saying, "It's not fair, Lord. It's not fair. We almost had him. We almost had him, Lord. Why would You show me this little boy and have me help him if You were going to take him?"

And the Lord spoke to me; He was so good, and He was so kind. He said, "Leanna, he's My little boy. He's My little boy and now he does have a family. He's never going to be alone again. He's not going to be hurt again. He's not sad anymore. He is where you're going to be."

I said, "Okay, Lord, I understand that."

I understood that. It was just one of the most gracious things that God has ever done for me and had spoken to me. Jimmy has forever changed the way I see things and think about things.

CHURCH, SCHOOL, WATER WELL

Now, fast-forward to the other side of the nation where I have a school for kids there on the 20 acres that we bought on that same trip.

We built a church, a school, and a water well. There is a really long story behind all of that. We continue to go back to that village, and our school is huge.

When we first started, we asked the kids, "What do you want to be when you grow up?" That's an American question asked of every kid, even teenagers and some adults. These kids didn't have an answer for us. They were young and had no idea of anything outside of farming. I had no idea that was the case.

The land we bought is at the bottom of a mountain. At the top of the mountain is where the witch doctor would take kids and make child sacrifices. I didn't know that at the time either, but this was a place that God said, "I want it redeemed. There have been too many kids' sacrifices and too much blood spilled on these children. These are My kids, and I want a future and a hope here."

We started going to this village quite often with my team of friends—Lisa, Mendy, Darrell, and with Troy. We poured into these kids. We gave them a really good education. They started reading books—they had never even seen books before. Then they started dreaming and saying things like, "I want to be a pilot, I want to be a doctor," "I want to be a pastor," "I am going to be a hairdresser." They also started having visions that they never had before because they didn't know there was anything else. They didn't know there was an opportunity to be anybody or anything other than working in the field. So now they have hope for a bright future.

Fast-forward again and now there is a young man who was just a little bitty guy when he came to us at the same time I lost Jimmy. He is now in school to be a heart surgeon. That is redemption.

Jimmy's story continues. He was a seed that went into the ground, and there is much fruit being produced from his life of faith, his life of believing, and his life of trusting in Jesus. Jimmy has been with his Lord and Savior for a long time, and he no longer suffers, he's no longer alone, he's part of a family, he's loved, and he is so well taken care of. He is better cared for than I could have ever have done for him. That's what God does.

Because of Jimmy, when God sends me and the team, we go praying.

That is Jimmy's story.

Purchase of First Land in Uganda

We had been doing ministry in Uganda for five or six years. On one of my trips there, we were going from village to village ministering. Then we came to one village that was on the opposite side of where I usually work.

Pastor David, who was taking us around, said we were going to stop there and do children's ministry. It was under a tree in a remote village on a dirt road. While we were ministering to the kids, all these people, mostly adults, started showing up. It was a bit eerie because there weren't any houses around that we could see, and we were in the jungle. They wanted us to minister to them, and at the time, I didn't do adult ministry; I did kids' ministry. Troy did adult ministry, and I did kids' ministry, and that worked great for both of us.

Pastor David did some ministry with the adults who came; then he said they wanted to hear me speak because they had never seen a white person. I spoke to them, and then we ministered to them. We prayed for this lady who had been completely bent over for most of her life. There are no schools out there, and the children go to work in the gardens from the time they are very young. She was stuck in that bent-over position and couldn't stand up. I prayed for her, and the power of prayer there was incredible.

We went for a couple of days in a row and did ministry in that same area. While going back on the third day, Pastor David told me that the people were asking where they should go to church. There are no churches in that area, only mosques. He asked me, "Do they go back to the mosque until we get a church?"

I'm thinking, *Why are you asking me? I don't live here. I don't know what we should do.* But I said, "Well, I guess we build a church."

And he said, "Okay, we'll build a church."

WE'LL BUILD A CHURCH

When we reached the place where the people were that day, Pastor David told them we were going to build a church for them. They asked where we were going to build it. A lady who was standing nearby said, "My husband owns this land, and we will sell you the front five acres."

I said, "Well, okay, that is amazing. How much money?"

She said, "He will sell it to you for two thousand dollars." At that time, we were so poor that we only had electricity some of the time. We definitely couldn't afford anything extra. But I said, "Okay. Yes." That was the beginning of all my yeses.

We decided we were going to do it. I didn't know how, but I just knew we were going to do it. I was going to call friends and get the money together to do this. I knew that we had to build this church. These people can't go back to the mosque.

Then I went to meet with the man who owned the land. He hadn't been to any of our "tree meetings." He was a Muslim man.

He walked out of his home, and a woman walked with him. I didn't recognize the woman who was walking with him. He said, "I was going to sell you 5 acres for $2,000, but I'm going to sell you 20 acres for $5,000."

I'm thinking, *You really don't know how to do math. That's really bad math.* But I decided not to point out his bad math. I almost wanted to feel badly about his bad math, but instead I said, "Yes! We will take it."

He said, "I don't believe in your God, but my wife has been bent over for many, many years, and you prayed for her, and she is healed." The reason I didn't recognize the woman with him was because now she was standing up straight. The man said, "If you will do this today, I will sell you this land."

He said, "I don't believe in your God, but my wife has been bent over for years, and you prayed for her, and she is healed."

I called Troy to tell him. It was during church service back in Texas. I said, "Troy, I got a really good sale!" I knew he was probably thinking, *Great, she's bringing home more shoes.* "Listen, this man is selling me 20 acres of land for $5,000." I imagined he was thinking, *Where is she coming up with this $5,000?* But he said, "Okay. That's great! That's so great, Leanna." We had friends who pitched in and helped; they got behind the vision and pitched in because God was just waiting for a *Yes!*

Now we own 75 acres there; we bought up all the land. We built the church and we have a school there for more than a thousand kids. That's where we put our first water well. That was our first school; and now we have forever homes there as well. That is where it all started.

SECTION THREE

The Door Is Open

But I Need My Spanx to Fit Through It

If you have really experienced the Anointed One,

and heard his truth, it will be seen in your life;

for we know that the ultimate reality is embodied in Jesus!

He has taught you to let go of the lifestyle of the ancient man,

the old self-life, which was corrupted by sinful and deceitful desires

that spring from delusions.

Now it's time to be made new by

every revelation that's been given to you.

Ephesians 4:21-23 TPT

9

Fitting Through His Doors

God opens doors for us that we must walk through. There are times when we can't fit through those doors. What keeps us from fitting through the door isn't necessarily that we are physically too big; but many times, it's because we're emotionally too big. What I mean by that can be seen in several ways. It may be there is a spirit of pride keeping you from humbling yourself to make it through the door that is open for you. Maybe you have regret, maybe you have self-doubt, maybe you are not confident, or you don't believe what God says is true. Maybe it's the big bags that you're carrying with you through life.

Whether a divorce, a childhood trauma, mistakes you've made, or something from our past that we have bagged up and carry with us, those things can keep us from entering into the life God has opened for us. I'm not discounting any of those things; however, the Lord asked us to give all that to Him and to trust Him. We can trust Him with everything about our lives. We can trust Him with our hurt; we can trust Him with the shame we are carrying.

The devil comes to steal, kill, and destroy. He is the accuser of believers (Revelation 12:10). The Lord doesn't accuse us. The Lord will confront us in those areas, but He confronts us so that we can be set free. He wants us to let it go and give it to Him so we aren't carrying all this stuff that keeps us from moving forward.

Many times, to be able to fit through the door God has opened for you, you have to get still, and you have to get small. There's a Scripture about the camel fitting through the eye of the needle (Matthew 19:24), which is a picture of a small opening in a city's wall that is a little door. The camel has to kneel down and crawl through it to be able to go through the wall and enter into the city. Before it can go through, all the bags that are loaded on the camel must be removed so it can fit through the opening.

Sometimes we have to get humble to be able to fit through these open doors. We may have to acknowledge that it may not be the way we think it should be; it may not look the way we think it should look. Being able to humble yourself and say, "Okay, God, I really do believe that You love me with all Your heart. I believe Your intentions for me are good. I believe Your heart toward me is good."

The Scripture says that He has plans for us and that they are for our good (Jeremiah 29:11). Sometimes we forget that; therefore, we think we have to protect ourselves. Protecting ourselves from Jesus is never the right answer. It's a lie; it's a trick and a deception.

Protecting ourselves from Jesus is never the right answer.

Anytime you spend time talking to the devil, you are deceived. He is a master craftsman in his wording and his deception. If you spend time rebuking him, talking to him, or whatever it is—stop now. You need to talk to Jesus. You need to spend your time counseling with the Father—not looking at what the enemy is doing, he is a distraction. He wants to distract you.

You have probably seen drivers being distracted by their cell phones. Sometimes, they are reading texts or emails while driving, or they're talking to somebody on the phone. The other day, I was driving down the road and saw something I had never seen before in all of my almost 60 years. There was a lady driving down the busy highway—while she was FaceTiming somebody. I could tell because her cell phone was located on her dashboard, and she was FaceTiming and using sign language while going really fast. If that's not distracted driving I don't know what is. That's crazy. Pull over and talk if it's that necessary. If not, then wait. Who knows what could happen? She was not only endangering her own life, but also endangering other people's lives.

I'm not going to say I'm guilt-free while driving, because I do get distracted extremely easily, and I know that I do. So I have to remind myself to stay focused. Likewise, I need to focus on what it is God has spoken to me. I need to focus on what it is He said for me to do. I need to humble myself when He has said for me to humble myself.

A lot of times, the baggage we carry is unforgiveness. You need to know that unforgiveness is a sin. It's not about your right to hold something against somebody. Unforgiveness is a sin. Jesus told us we have to forgive if we're going to be forgiven (Matthew 6:15). Sin isn't a list of dos and don'ts. It's not rights and wrongs that are accounted to us. Sin is anything that separates us from the love of

God. If you have unforgiveness, you are separated from the love of God.

Unforgiveness is a sin that will keep you from your Father's heart. It will keep you from fitting through that door of opportunity, that door of progression, that door of promotion that God has for you. It will keep you from going into those good places where He wants to take you. It's not that He doesn't want to take you there. He's opened the door; He's done everything He can do. But you have to take on the responsibility of getting yourself through that door.

He gives us different keys in our lives, and those keys open doors. Those keys are the anointing that He has put upon our life. I like to call them our superpowers. That's probably not a religiously correct term. But everybody has superpowers and the fun thing about superpowers is you don't even know it's your superpower. It is just normal to you.

Some people have the superpower of organization, which is not my gifting. I have a daughter-in-law who has a superpower of organization, and I have to call upon that superpower quite often to help me. I love things very clean, and I love them organized, but I'm not an organizer. I can't put things in order. My mind doesn't work like that. It's frustrating to me when I can't seem to get it in order.

But once it's done, I can keep it organized. I know that sounds so crazy because I am a clean freak. But those are two different skills. She doesn't see it as a superpower, but it is. To be able to organize is her anointing.

Most of the anointings you have in the natural are just types and shadows of what you have in the spirit. God has given us the ability to see the things naturally that are happening supernaturally. You have to be able to see into both of those realms and not take everything as if it's just normal. I sometimes do that, too, because it's just normal to me. People asked me to tell different stories they had heard about my life. I didn't realize that was a story because, to me, it's just normal.

As mentioned previously, because of the way I grew up with so many kids sharing my parents, people ask if that bothered me. No, it never bothered me. It was normal because that's how I grew up, and that's what I knew. I thought everybody looked like that. I didn't notice any difference.

When we rescue kids, oftentimes they don't know that they need to be rescued until after the fact, after they are healed, after they are set free—because that life was normal to them, and they didn't know anything could be different.

It's so hard to explain this aspect of life to people when trying to help them out of a bad situation. For example, if they've been addicted to drugs their whole life, all they know is *that* feeling; they don't know anything different. So helping them break out of addiction and dealing with real-life issues sober, won't feel normal to them. To them, addiction is normal, so they think they are supposed to feel like that. They think they are supposed to be depressed and need drugs to be able to get through each day.

When they are set free, truly set free, and can fit through the door that God has opened for them, they are amazed. Going through God's open door takes them to deliverance and to the ability to live life more abundantly. When they get to the other side of it, they see that they had no idea how downtrodden they were—no idea how close to death they were. They didn't know because an unhealthy lifestyle became normal to them—a lifestyle that was never meant to be normal.

YOUR OWN FIT

Likewise in the spiritual realm of life, you may not always feel as if you fit through God's open door. For example, when you have an anointing in your life and you don't realize it is an anointing, it's easy to look enviously at someone else's anointing. This is why the Scriptures say not to envy what other people have. When we get into envy, it's easier to see their superpower, their gifting, or whatever it is, than it is for us to see our own anointing and recognize it. When that happens, we start to want what someone else has. We want to preach like that person, so we study them, we copy them, and then pretty soon, we become jealous of them.

When you become jealous, you start tearing that person down. That is not a Kingdom mindset; it is not part of the Kingdom of God. If you're in a place where you want to judge everybody and everything around you, that's not Kingdom thinking. That attitude is from the kingdom of the enemy, not the Kingdom of God. You have to be very careful not to fall into the enemy's trap of envy. You have to judge yourself in that place. Ask yourself: Am I an example of living in God's Kingdom, or have I fallen into the enemy's kingdom?

THE LORD'S SIDE

I love, love, love Joshua. What a warrior, what a hero! That man's superpower was that he was a warrior. He was in the Promised Land near Jericho, and he was walking through the doors that God called him to walk through. He was doing what God had anointed him to do and called him to do. He was doing all of it with all of his heart. He was doing this with all his might.

In Joshua 5:13-15, the Bible tells us that while he was following God's plan, an angel showed up on the battlefield. Joshua had been on the battlefield for a long time, defeating the enemies of God. When Joshua saw the angel, he went to him and said, "Whose side are you on? Are you on our side, or are you on the enemy's side?"

I love what the angel said to him, "Neither side. I am on the side of the Lord."

That answer was so brilliant—we need to be on the side of the Lord. Even though Joshua was fighting for the Lord and fighting those battles, this angel (the commander of the Lord's army) was not on either side. This angel was sent to be on the Lord's side and fight what God called him to fight.

When I read what the angel said, it reminded me of a time when we were first in ministry. I grew up in church, and I had a super good dad. He passed away some years ago. I didn't realize the anointing he had in his life, I thought it was just his weirdness or quirkiness. Now that I'm older and understand the supernatural and the prophetic much better than I did back then, I know he was anointed.

When I was growing up, the "prophetic" was when a prophet came to church, or someone would stand up in the middle of a service and prophesy. Usually the person spoke a word of judgment, a word of encouragement, or whatever, and it was just one word for everybody. It was a blanket word; not unique for a specific person.

My dad had a prophetic anointing, and we didn't know it because we didn't understand what it was. Now that I'm older and think back on all of what he said, I realize that he was so right on.

I was a young woman in ministry, and we were going through a very hard time in ministry. I remember going to him and saying,

"Dad, this is what happened. It's not fair; I don't know what to do." I was pouring my heart out and he stopped me.

He said, "There are three sides to every story. When he said that, I thought, *Oh, great, he's gonna say something crazy like he always does.* He said, "There's your side, there's their side, and then there's the truth."

I told him that wasn't helping me right now. I said, "I need you to hear me; I need you to be on my side on this; I need you to tell me I'm right." I knew I was right, but it wasn't about being right. Of course, my dad was actually right.

Dad said, "You need to stick to truth. Jesus is the truth, He's the way, He's the truth, and He's life. If you don't stick with the truth, it doesn't matter if you're right or wrong. You have to stick with the truth. That's the only thing that lasts."

At that moment a big paradigm shift happened for me. I stopped taking sides, taking my own side, and actually expecting people to take sides.

Because of that wise lesson from my dad and the words of that angel, I tend to look at the Lord whenever a division of some sort comes up. I tell Him, "Lord, I can't see the whole picture of all of this. I can only see what I can see in the natural; but Lord, You see things from a supernatural point of view. You know the beginning and the end. You know the ins and the outs, and even more than that, You know people's hearts. I might not be judging the situation right, but You know, and I'm going to lean into the Holy Spirit and ask You to lead me and guide me even if it doesn't make sense to my natural being."

I have done that throughout the years. I'm still growing, and I'm not quite there completely, but walking through that door opened a great sense of freedom for me. I no longer had to depend on my emotions and my ability to see what was right in front of me, or what I had decided was right or wrong. It was the angel standing before me saying, "I'm not on your side, I'm not on their side. I'm on the side of the Lord."

Be on the side of the Lord. Don't make people choose sides. If other people do that, then that's on them, and the Lord can deal with them. But you choose this day to serve the Lord. That's what Joshua did, and that's what he said, "...As for me and my house, we will serve the Lord" (Joshua 24:15 NKJV). What a hero. What a rockstar.

It is very important to know that whenever you are discovering your gifts and your talents, they may just seem normal and easy for you. Some people are gifted learners. They can read a book and remember exactly what was written. They know how to implement or use the knowledge to their advantage. Then there are others of us who have to touch it and feel it, smell it, and taste it to figure out what's going on. Those are two different giftings, so don't be upset at the gifting you have or be jealous of the gifting someone else has.

For example, people with curly hair want straight hair; if they have straight hair, they want curly hair. People who are thin want to be heavier. If they're heavy they want to be skinny. Whatever it is, we want something different from how God wonderfully made us. He made us in His image.

Anytime the devil comes to you and says you're just not enough—you're not smart enough, good enough, you don't have enough money, you don't have enough this or that, you don't have enough charisma, you don't have what it takes for whatever it is— remember, he's a liar.

YOU'RE MORE THAN ENOUGH

The Lord says that with Him you're more than enough. You don't need anything but the Lord on your side. When He's on your side, there's nothing that can come against you. I learned that truth throughout my almost 35 years of ministry. I have had to learn it over and over and over. I think, *Okay, this is it, I'm sinking this time. There's no recovery for this ship that's going to the bottom of the ocean. Then all of a sudden, the life preservers come out, and "tadah!" I'm facing a bigger, more beautiful, incredible thing than I could've ever hoped or dreamed.*

Sometimes what we believe is normal has to die in order for us to really live an abundant life. It seems like this doesn't make sense, and it doesn't always make sense in the natural because it's not natural. It's supernatural. The Lord is supernatural, and we can't put Him in a natural space. He does things that are so different and so contrary to how we would do it or how we think it should be done. But we must always remember that He is faithful, and He's good.

Sometimes I get to places where I think, *I can't get past this. I can't. I can't do this anymore.* In some of those times I have told the Lord that I quit. I think, *I quit. I can't do this anymore because it hurts too bad.* Usually when it hurts, it's not me who is hurting, it's someone I love who is hurting. I love them too much to see them in pain. That's when I cry out, "My God, I can't do this anymore." And He always stands with me and tells me I can. He reminds me I can do whatever comes along. He says, "You can do this; not only can you do this, but we're going to do this together." He never leaves us or forsakes us, never.

Whenever the devil is telling you that you are not enough, it's actually quite the opposite. He knows that you're more than enough to do whatever needs to be done. He knows your anointing. He knows what your calling is. He knows what your superpowers are that he wants to blind you from. Ask the Lord to show you where you are anointed and to show you where you are gifted.

Troy is very much a people person. I am an introvert who is very outgoing and adventurous, so people mistake that for being an extrovert. Whereas Troy is very much an extrovert, I am not so much. Troy is a very touchy-feely person. I grew up in a very loving home where we loved each other, but we kept our hands to ourselves. So it wasn't a very touchy-feely family. You could tell we loved each other, but we didn't touch each other, we didn't hug each other. We didn't do that because there were so many of us. We had lots of rules that we had to follow to keep the order in our house and keeping your hands to yourself was one of them.

Because Troy is a very huggy-feely person, everybody started adapting to that culture. It took me a long time before I was okay with people hugging me all the time. Now, of course, I realize that is part of my gifting. The Lord showed me that the devil tried to use against me what is actually my superpower. At first, I thought people were just being nice to me. But then I heard over and over from people that getting a hug from me impacted them. Some said it made them feel like I was their mom or that it changed their life, and it really made a difference.

Then one day after hearing it over and over and still thinking they said it because it was something nice to say, the Lord told me that wasn't the case. He told me it was an anointing He had given me. He said He had given me an anointing of hugging people and making a difference. It breaks the yokes. It shares the love of the Father with them in a way they never knew. Had I not broken through that childhood tradition and not submitted myself and put on my Spanx to get through that door, I would have missed using my gifting. And other people would have missed receiving what God had for them because I wasn't willing to be transformed by the renewing of my mind (Romans 12:2).

If you want to fit through the door, you have to let the Lord transform you by renewing your mind. You have to think differently; you have to act differently. You have to believe differently—you have to let go of some of the traditions you learned when growing up, and the things that make sense to you that are culturally acceptable.

You have to be like Jesus. If you hear the Father say it, you have to do it. If you hear the Father say it, you have to speak it. The only way you can do that and do it right is to: 1) practice it; and 2) listen to Him. You have to turn off all the other voices. Turn off the ones in your head that tell you this or tell you that. Turn off the voice of the enemy who's coming against you. Don't listen to the culture that's coming against you or the fear that comes against you. You have to come against all those things. You have to say, "Okay, God, I'm tuning in to hear *Your* voice and Your voice alone. You're going to walk me through this, and it's gonna be better than what I could've hoped or imagined."

The breakthroughs you will see in your life and in your family and in your ministry are going to be astronomical, because you're going to be walking in the anointing. The superpower God has given you will break the yokes, set the captive free, and bring healing to people. You can't give what you don't have to give. The Lord has to heal you; He has to transform you. He has to anoint you in these places. You have to be comfortable and confident in His goodness, and you have to trust Him.

I talked about trust in Chapter 4. Trust is a big deal. If you're going to love, you have to trust. You have to trust God. He loves you, He trusts you. He trusts you with the anointing He gave you. If you're a parent, He trusts you with the children He gave you. If you're married, He trusts you with the spouse He gave you. He trusts you to love them, to encourage them, to see the best in them.

If you're married, it is so important that you speak goodness and encouragement into your spouse. If you're a wife, you need to be speaking into your husband by faith. Speak, "You are a mighty man." It doesn't matter what his actions or reactions are or what he is doing right now. When you speak life into him, you will reap life. But if you speak condemnation, if you speak judgment, if you speak criticism to him, guess what, you're going to get exactly that in return.

The same applies to your children. You have to speak life into them; encourage them, love them, hug them. I'm not saying you don't discipline or that you don't correct their behavior. You do, but you do it with life. Never partner with the enemy, and never bring shame to people. The Lord doesn't shame us. He always encourages us. He brings us opportunities to change us and to transform us, but He doesn't shame us.

FORGIVENESS AND MERCY

Repentance is the greatest gift that God has given us. When He exposes sin in your life, the best reaction is to run to King Jesus and say to Him, "I'm a mess." Tell Him that you're a mess and that you made a bad choice. Tell Him, "I would rather trust in Your judgment than in all of the enemies around me." He's a good God. He's a good Father. You may get a spanking as a consequence, because God will not be mocked. What you sow is what you're going to reap.

But the reaping that comes from the Lord is full of mercy and full of grace. It actually elevates you and takes you to a place where you could never have gone if you had not walked through that challenge. God will let you walk through the hard circumstances that seem so wrong and so messed up. It's in those times when God will tell you that He is allowing you these experiences as they are opportunities for you to gain wisdom and knowledge and mercy.

There are often times when people who are the biggest mess will come into our lives. They hurt us the worst, and they are the most offensive to us. They have done damage to us, to our family, to our hearts, and God said that He wants us to give mercy to that person in our life. Our response can be, "That's impossible, God. Do You see what they've done? Do You hear what they've said? There's no way I can give mercy. There's no way I can even work on this whole forgiveness thing because it's just too much. It's too much how they betrayed me, how they hurt me, how they let me down, the things they said about me—it is all just too much."

Yet the Lord tells you that you really need this opportunity to be merciful. "This is an opportunity that I am letting you walk through because you need the opportunity to bank some mercy in your life. There's going to come a time when you're going to need people to show you mercy. You will have that deposit in your bank account, or you won't. You need a bank account full of mercy, forgiveness, love, and hope." All these gifts God gives us when He brings us into these situations that are sometimes hard to understand.

We may cry out to Him and ask, "Why are You putting me through this? I have been good my whole life. I don't deserve this, and it's not fair." These type of reactions prove our immaturity. But our good Lord will tell us we are looking at the circumstances wrongly. When you're going through difficult times, see them as opportunities for you to deposit all you can into your spiritual bank account—these are the riches of His glory. This is the wisdom you gain and will need tomorrow.

The keys He's given us are so important. But we have to use them to open the right doors and walk through them. When we do, we walk through them with the wisdom and the grace and the glory He gives us.

But you have to be wearing your Spanx to fit through some of these doors. I know I do. Sometimes I have to say, "Okay, Lord, I'm a little bit too big for my britches here, and I can't fit through the door anymore. I'm going to have to leave this baggage behind. I'm going to have to leave this sorrow back there. I'm going to have to change the way I think about this thing from the past. I'm going to have to change the way I think about this person because it's easier for me to not like the person than to forgive. Lord, I'm going to have to move into a new place of maturity with You and see situations and people as Jesus saw them."

I can't even imagine that when He was on the Cross, Jesus said, *"Father, forgive them; for they know not what they do"* (Luke 23:34 KJV). That is mind-blowing to me. It's mind-boggling to me they shamed Jesus, the greatest of all people in the whole universe. And yet He lay down His life for us—for each and every one of us. And all of us are in the same place as those people who stood there looking at Him naked. They were shaming Him and mocking Him. What a horrible scene—but He hung there with His arms spread wide before the Father and said, *"Forgive them, for they know not what they do."*

Can you forgive the people who have shamed you and wronged you? Can you forgive the people you've laid down your life for, the very people you have sacrificed everything you have to love? Can you forgive them when they turn on you, beat you, and publicly shame you? Can you go before the Father and say, "Father, forgive them, for they know not what they do"? That's a hard one; that is the hard, hard door to go through.

But if you're going to go through the doors God opens that no one can close, you have to be able to forgive. You have to forfeit your pride, your judgment, and your regrets to walk through and take hold of all that God has waiting for you.

The Lord says to us:

> *And be not conformed to this world: but be ye transformed by the renewing of your mind, that ye may prove what is that good, and acceptable, and perfect, will of God* (Romans 12:2 KJV).

10

Jewish Jesus

I am a hands-on learner. Rather than reading about a subject and totally understanding it, I need to touch it, feel it, and taste it. I learned how to learn in other ways, but I was definitely a very visual learner.

When I was growing up, I heard the Scriptures all the time, but some of what I heard just didn't make sense to me. I'm one of the ones the parables are for. I get those. When I read about what Jesus says the Kingdom of Heaven is like and He gives an illustration, my response is, *Oh, that makes so much sense.* His parables give me a visual understanding because of the way they are written. I love parables.

I also love traveling so I can actually see what people are telling me about. I can read about other places and get them in my head; but when I travel there, I have those *Ah, now I see* moments.

I always wanted to go to Israel because I love the Bible, I love Jesus, and I love the church. I love everything about it. It's my inheritance; it's my heritage. Growing up, I loved Missionary Sunday. All the missionaries would come to church, and I could see their clothes, hear how they talked, and hear about the food they ate. Even though I was never going to eat any of their food because I am a super picky eater, it was still very interesting to me.

Going to Israel was a gift that God waited a while to give me. I went to many other places before I visited Israel. When I did get to go there, everything changed for me. It changed how I saw the Bible. All of a sudden, walking down the Via Delarosa, going to Golgotha, going to the Garden of Gethsemane, in the middle of all of it, I thought, *Jesus was a Jew!*

Jesus's culture was so different from anything I knew. I had only known the "California Jesus" and the "Texas Jesus." I didn't know the "Jewish Jesus." I didn't know His culture. I thought He conformed His life to my image, instead of me conforming my life to His image. This realization was a whole paradigm shift for me.

I had the Christian picture in my mind of what Jesus looked like. At this point, I didn't understand the Orthodox Jews; I didn't understand who the Messianic Jews were, other than I knew they loved Jesus. I didn't know about the secular Jewish people. I didn't know anything about their culture other than Jesus came from Israel. That's all I knew.

When Troy and I walked off the plane in Israel, I was so excited to be there. We were going through customs, which was no easy feat, when I saw an Orthodox Jew. He was wearing a black hat and had Hasidic curls. He looked the way I was expecting everybody to look. It was like people who visit Texas for the first time expecting to see most people wearing cowboy hats on horseback.

Seeing this man, I said to Troy, "I bet that's what Jesus looked like." Troy smiled a little and said, "Well, maybe." He was looking at me as if he wasn't sure if I was serious or not. He is very gracious.

After leaving the customs area, we saw that same man sitting outside on the curb, drinking from a whisky bottle and smoking a cigarette. Troy said, "I don't think that's what Jesus looked like." We started laughing and I said, "Well, I *did* think that was what Jesus looked like, but maybe not."

So the first thing that happened when in Israel was that the image I held of what Jesus looked like was shattered. That was *not* what Jesus looked like, and now the Lord could show me what He wanted me to understand about Jesus.

That started our journey into Israel. I loved that trip. It was amazingly beautiful and absolutely breathtaking. We went with quite a few pastors and saw many of the holy sites and experienced the holy walk as do all the pilgrims of today. It was a dream come true.

Since I am a very visual learner, being in Israel helped me in my journey I have walked all the years with the Lord to understand the Scriptures even better. Seeing the sites made the Bible come to life. I understood the culture and what the Scriptures were referring to once I could see it and touch and feel it.

The visit also gave me a heart for the people. Not just the Jewish people but the Gentiles as well. It opened my heart to the religious people, the secular people, the Messianic people, and all the Christian people. The people as a whole who live in Israel are a beautiful, incredible group of people. It was a privilege to be there.

When I saw the whitewashed sepulchers, I remembered the Scripture: *"Woe unto you, scribes and Pharisees, hypocrites! for ye are like unto whited sepulchres, which indeed appear outward, but are within full of dead men's bones, and of all uncleanness"* (Matthew 23:27 KJV). The verse made so much sense to me when I actually saw the sepulchers. The religious leaders were keeping their outside looking clean, but inside they were not alive to God. The meaning is so much clearer when I delved into Middle Eastern Jewish culture with people who are actually from there.

We returned to Israel again, this time with the Father's House ministry located in Cleburne, Texas. We met Ron and Elana Cantor and their three beautiful girls, Sharon, Gaelle, and Danielle. We connected with them as ministry partners and have been friends with them ever since. I have visited Israel several times since then and enjoyed the festivals and holidays.

Traveling worldwide is a gift God has given to us. He has connected us with indigenous people from the countries where we work. God has done that from the beginning of our time in Israel; we are connected to the Jewish people. Some of the most incredible friends we have to this day are true Jewish people from Israel. I have learned so much more about Jesus, the culture He came from, and the setting of the Bible. Knowing what I do now, the Bible is a completely different book for me. It all makes so much more sense. Instead of trying to bring Jesus into my American culture, I actually understand the culture in which He was living and teaching while on earth. I get so much more out of God's Word now.

GOD'S WORD

I'm finishing my Doctorate Degree in Theology, and in the Ministry class, one of my professors said we could only use the *Complete Jewish Bible* as a biblical reference. I grew up reading only the *King James Version*; that was the only version I knew. Since I have been in school, I have used a variety of Bibles that other professors required. But when I read the *Complete Jewish Bible*, I thought it made so much more sense. After all, Jesus was Jewish, Mary was Jewish, and all the people we read about in the Bible were Middle Easterners from Middle Eastern culture.

Their culture really hasn't changed that much—most remain true to their culture. Our Western culture has changed because people from all around the world come to the United States and bring their culture with them. That is beautiful. But it is also beautiful to see the Jewish culture. The Middle East is very different from what we know in the West. Unless you are studying the Bible from that perspective, you won't get the full picture.

I have had the privilege of being friends and sisters with my dear Elana, whom I love. As I've come to know her experiences, I have seen the Father's heart and the Lord's heart for His people through her eyes. She was born in that region of the world and grew up in Jerusalem. She is 100 percent Jewish, a Moroccan Jew. She is absolutely beautiful. I also met her mother and her family and have had the experience of visiting with them in that great nation.

I love that God had Jesus born as a Jew and made that very real to us so that we could search out the matter. I now understand what it means to have a king and a judge over a people group, and I understand how disputes among the countries work. Even now in our headlines we are reading about these traditions and cultures, but as Westerners we don't have the full understanding of what is going on in the Middle East because the culture there is so very different from ours.

Understanding the Jewish culture has been really good for me; it's been a blessing to delve into the customs and beliefs of Jewish Jesus, and I love Him even more. I love everything about Him. I love the culture over there. I love their understanding of family. There is a different meaning of the family in the Jewish culture than anywhere else.

For example, during their Shabbat dinner, everyone focuses on each other. All technology is turned off. Whether you are a secular

Jew or an Orthodox Jew, Shabbat Shalom means family time. It is a time to rest and have a meal together. And that meal takes hours from start to finish.

Shabbat Shalom is their family time. It is a time to rest and spend hours around the table as a celebration of family.

The Shabbat dinner is not about going through the fast-food place and eating in the car on the way home so they can binge on Netflix. No. They spend hours around the table as a family. They tell jokes and talk about what happened that week. If there was a conflict, they lay that aside. There are no unsettling issues brought to the table. This table is a weekly celebration, every week after week. That was an interesting insight for me.

Christians are all looking forward to the marriage supper of the Lamb. Yet as people who are not from that culture, we have no idea what we are actually looking forward to—but these people have an understanding what the supper will be like.

We went with Elana to a Moroccan Jewish wedding in Israel, and it blew my mind. I now have so much more understanding of what a celebration it will be as we stand before the Lord as His bride, and He is so excited as the Groom to receive us. The party afterward is a huge all-day event where everyone comes together to celebrate the marriage. That is what we have to look forward to. But unless we know Jesus's roots and what He comes from, we won't have a good grasp of the important details.

People research their ancestry to discover and understand who their generational family is, which is good. Likewise, we need to know who our Savior's generational family is and understand that He is Jewish. We have no reason to be ashamed of His heritage or try to hide that fact. We need to embrace it.

Because Jesus is our Husband, our Groom, and we are His bride, that makes us part of the Jewish family, too. As a church, we need to remember that. We need to stand with Israel—our family, our people, God's people.

THE LIVING BIBLE

Incredibly, I had the opportunity to tour Boaz's threshing floor, which I had never even dreamed that was possible, but God gave that gift to me. It was a very special experience, and one of the greatest personal treasures from the Lord. He allowed me to experience all the emotions that were stirred up from being in the place where my favorite story in the Bible occurred.

I have also worshiped while on the Sea of Galilee and in all parts of that incredible nation. I've met and talked with many people. I loved them and poured into the people as they have poured into me and loved me.

On the last trip I took to Israel, I went with several of my girl-friends. While we were there, we went to the Wailing Wall. That particular day was a special day for *bar mitzvah,* young men who were going through their rite of passage were at the Wall, celebrating. They read from the Torah; all Jews, whether Orthodox or not, learn the Torah.

If you go to Israel, don't miss touring Yad Vashem, The World Holocaust Remembrance Center in Jerusalem. It was emotionally hard for me seeing the faces and reading about the millions of Jews who were murdered during World War II. As I walked through the hallways, a voice was saying, "We will not forget. We will not forget." That is one of the commandments of the Lord.

Jewish people know the Torah, know who they are, and know where they come from. It goes back to identity. They know who they are because they don't forget! Their mantra, "We will never forget" is from the Father's heart.

On a trip to Argentina many years ago, the Lord gave me the phrase, "Don't forget." There are things we are supposed to remember. We are supposed to remember the goodness of God in the land of the living. We are supposed to remember His promises. We are to always remember His covenant with us.

But we are also supposed to remember our covenant to Him and our promises to Him. These are what connect us with Him in His heart. We are to remember what He has done for us. Those are our testimonies. Never forget who He is to you and the incredible work He has done in your life. Don't get distracted by the struggles; don't be distracted by the fight or the circumstances—look at each as opportunities God has given you to strengthen your soul.

Being able to see the bar mitzvah celebration at the Temple Wall was amazing. The young men were celebrating on our side of the wall, and the rest of the families were on the other side. The moms and sisters and grandmas were all there. Their celebration of these men reading the Torah was beautiful and spiritually significant for each young man. God has given me so many beautiful memories of Israel, of His Promised Land to His chosen people.

Israel is an incredible, flourishing land full of milk and honey, just like the Lord promised. But just because a people are blessed and living in a land of milk and honey, doesn't mean they don't fight battles. The lessons I have learned by going there and being part of that beautiful nation have given me greater resilience in my walk. Knowing those people are His children, His chosen people, and His chosen nation reveals so much insight into Father God. The Jews have been fighting battles for centuries, and we can see how God strengthens them to fight against the enemy.

I have experienced being in that great nation that has been continually persecuted by so many nations for so long. Yet the resilience to hold on and the gratitude they have toward their nation, toward one another, and toward God is inspiring. Whether they believe there is a Jesus or not, they really do love God. There is a remnant in Israel who do know Jesus as the Messiah. All those people are His people called by His name. Those are His people, and He is coming back for them, just like He is coming back for you and me.

We have been grafted into that body; I am forever so grateful to our Jewish brothers and sisters who have welcomed us into the family and have loved us. I'm grateful for that great nation. I pray for the peace of Jerusalem; but more than that, I pray for my brothers and sisters in Israel and around the world who have been persecuted their entire lives. I pray they will be at peace and remain resilient until the Lord comes for them, and for all of us. I'm grateful to be part of His family.

SECTION FOUR

Teach Me Your Ways, Oh Lord

Because I'm Lost Again

Direct me, Yahweh, throughout my journey

so I can experience Your plans for my life.

Reveal the life-paths that are pleasing to You.

Escort me into Your truth;

take me by the hand and teach me.

For you are the God of my salvation;

I have wrapped my heart into Yours all day long!

Psalm 25:4-5 TPT

11

Being Lost

The people in my life who know me well know that I am "navigationally challenged," to say the least. For example, when staying at a hotel, when I leave my room, I'm never sure which way to turn to get to the elevator. And after I find the elevator, when I walk out of the elevator, I always go in the wrong direction. I have even tried to trick myself and think, *Okay, it makes sense for me to go this way, so I'm going to go the opposite way because it's always the opposite way.* Nope, I still go the wrong direction. It's the craziest thing, and I've always been that way. I fight it, I hate it, but it is what it is. It's become a longstanding joke. If someone can get lost, it's me.

But I always seem to find my way, and I'll tell you how that happens—the Holy Spirit leads and guides my way. The Scripture even says so: *"the Spirit of the Truth, he will take you by the hand and guide you"* (John 16:13 The Message). He really and truly leads and guides our way. I have learned to be so codependent on the Holy Spirit, not just leading and guiding my way, but in every part of my everyday life.

For instance, I'll be in the grocery store walking up and down the aisles, and I'll see something random and think, *Huh, I don't need that, I have that.* Yet I pick it up and put it in the cart. When I get home, sure enough, I needed that particular item. In those moments the Holy Spirit is telling me something. And it's not necessarily because He's helping me with my grocery list, but He's helping me fine-tune my spiritual hearing and obeying.

He really and truly leads and guides our way.

I've noticed that has happened throughout my life in different areas. I will think something or go somewhere and see something, and it triggers me. And I have learned to be very, very intentional with that Voice and that feeling, knowing that the Holy Spirit is working in me. So if there's something I pick up but don't know why, I just go ahead and get it. And if it's a specific direction I'm supposed to be going toward, I'll just turn and go that way.

The other day I was returning home from an appointment, and I needed to fill up the car with gas. Well, the logical and quickest place was the gas station right next door to me, and I really needed to get gas. So I thought, *I'll go there.* But then I heard the Holy Spirit tell me, *No, I want you to go down to the grocery store and get gas.* It wasn't too far out of my way, but it was in the opposite direction. Because the Holy Spirit knows all things and is so smart and wise, as He says in Scripture, I went the way He told me. When I arrived, I saw an older man who had either Alzheimer's or dementia who really needed help. I would not have been able to help him if I had gone to the station near my house.

AROUND THE MOUNTAIN

I sometimes hear the Holy Spirit in the moments when it seems inconvenient or out of my way. But when you hear the Holy Spirit speak to you, you have to be quick to obey Him. After all, He is the best navigator in the world.

About 10 years ago, I had the privilege of taking quite a few students from our youth group on a senior trip. They wanted to go to Northern California, specifically to Bethel Church.

We flew into San Francisco and were going to stay up in Mount Shasta, which is beautiful, but a rather long drive. They wanted to see the redwood forest, so there was going to be a lot of driving up in the mountains around crazy curves in high altitudes, and no guardrails. So the whole trip was a little sketchy.

Anyway, I was driving a 15-passenger van, and had a navigator in the front seat across from me who was doing a great job. We had been on this road for about three hours, looking at the spectacular scenery and trying to get to our final destination. Then we came to a fork in the road. In my heart, I heard the Holy Spirit tell me, "You need to go left."

But the navigator was insistent that I go right. Several girls were already carsick because of the winding road and the high altitude. We were all really ready to get out of the car. We had been driving for over three hours, and now we were so far out in the country that, of course, the GPS didn't work. The navigator was looking at a real paper map, which is fine, because I can't read a map. So I submitted to the navigator, and turned right.

Doggone it, after about 30 minutes, I realized we were going in a big circle around this mountain, again. I could have screamed, I could have cried. I could have done all of those emotions along with all of the poor girls in the car who were carsick.

And, there was no way to turn around. So I said, "Lord, I don't even know what to do here other than go around this mountain again." Then I started thinking, *Holy Spirit, nothing goes to waste in Your Kingdom. I know that. And I know that this lesson is not going to waste. And I know that You're with us, and You lead us, and You guide us.* I should have gone with what I knew was right by the Holy Spirit. But I doubt myself because I'm so directionally challenged that I tend to lean on other people.

But, I'm *not* Holy Spirit challenged. I know when it's Him. I knew it was Him, and in hindsight, I knew I should have just gone with what I heard from Him. But, it is what it is—a lesson learned.

During that time, the Lord talked to me about mountains. I love, love mountains. I love the mountains across from the ocean. The views are just beautiful. I love the West Coast, which is where I grew up. It's stunning country. As I was driving through those mountains, around those curves with these girls, and listening to the Lord speak to me, He told me about mountains.

He showed me there are mountains that we go around, and if we don't listen to the Holy Spirit, we wind up going around that mountain more than once. Sometimes, we still don't listen. Then we go around that mountain again, and we go around that mountain again.

And then the Lord told me about the mountains in my personal life that I was going around. I was reminded of how frustrating it is.

We can blame other people, the navigators, the other voices in our life for going around those mountains, for giving us bad advice, or for whatever we want to blame them for. Ultimately, though, we're responsible for hearing the Holy Spirit and obeying Him.

He started talking to me about the mountains in my life, of times when I have relied on other opinions, other voices, and other people to help me navigate through situations.

One mountain was specifically about unforgiveness toward a group of people. I was having a really hard time getting past a terrible offense. And it wasn't the first time, it wasn't the second time, it wasn't even the third time, and it was the same offense. It really triggered me because I didn't understand how to get past it. "How do I forgive them again, Lord?" I know the Scriptures say 70 times seven. I knew all of that, but it didn't help in that situation. And the Lord just asked me a question. He said, "Are you tired of going around this mountain, Leanne? Are you really tired of it?"

My answer was, "Yes, Lord, I am tired of this mountain. Can I please get a different scenery going here?" So, I dealt with the unforgiveness toward those people with Him. I could see the situation from the Lord's perspective, not my own personal hurt, my own personal offenses, my own personal view of things. I saw it from God's view and His heart and understood better what was going on.

Yet, it didn't make the situation right. It still hurt, but I was able to forgive, truly forgive. I remember one day asking the Lord how I would know if I had truly forgiven them. To me, I thought forgiving them would make the situation better. Everything would be okay. It would be fixed, and healed, or whatever was needed. But that's not always the case.

And it wasn't the case in this situation. So I asked the Lord, "How do I know if I've really forgiven them? Am I just supposed to go over there and say, 'Hi,' like nothing had happened?"

In this instance, the hurt didn't come from our side. And even to this day, I can tell you it wasn't on our side. It was definitely something that had been done to us. And I didn't know what to do next. So I asked Him again, "Lord, am I supposed to go to them and say, 'I'm sorry'? Should I do that, even though I didn't do anything to them, just to try to make it better?"

That is what we have done in the past when faced with this circumstance.

And the Lord said, "No."

First He told me, "It's not about you anymore. You've done what you were supposed to do. You have truly forgiven, and now it's on them. Whatever they choose to do or not do is on them; it's none of your business anymore."

I asked the Lord, "So how do I know that I've truly forgiven them in this situation?"

He asked me to think about how I now feel about it all. He said, "You will know when you go to a store and see them, and you want to go the opposite direction, or you want to crawl into your shell like a turtle and act like you can't see them, or you completely ignore them and walk the other direction."

I said, "Yes, Lord. I do know that feeling."

He went on, "It is that sinking feeling like you're getting pulled over by the police and you've been speeding, and you're guilty. That's the same feeling."

I said, "Yes, Lord, I do know."

And He said, "When you see them and don't have that feeling anymore, you have truly forgiven them. When you don't feel like they owe you anything, they don't owe you an apology, that's when you know you have forgiven them."

So, one day I saw the person who had instigated most of the situation, and I didn't have that feeling anymore. I didn't want to be besties, but I didn't have that feeling of dread. I didn't have that anxiety. I didn't have that sinking feeling in my stomach. There really weren't a lot of feelings at all anymore. I was confident in myself and in this situation. I knew I had truly forgiven, and that was a mountain I no longer was going to have to go around again.

I was so grateful for the lesson I learned while driving around that mountain with the young girls. We only did it one more time. I didn't do it any additional times because we turned left at the fork in the road, just as the Holy Spirit told me to do the first time.

I'm ever so grateful for learning that lesson in my life.

He told me, "You have truly forgiven. Whatever they choose is on them. It's none of your business anymore."

CAST THE MOUNTAIN

Then the Lord started talking to me about other mountains—about mountains in the Bible and the different kinds of mountains in our lives. He says, "If you have enough faith, you can say to this mountain, 'Be moved,' and it'll be cast into the sea" (see Matthew 21:21).

I want you to especially know this:

> Most of our situations are just that—our personal, individual situations. They're in our head. There are battles we're fighting within ourselves over something we think we know, something we were sure we knew, something we think we understand, or we're confident we understand, and life's not the way we want it to be or we think it should be.
>
> Each of us have our own strifeful battles in our minds and hearts. Even if real and legitimate, the struggles can get out of hand. If we don't give them to the Lord, we're fighting battles we won't be able to win.

I say all that from so much experience on the battlefield. One particular day, I realized that I had been fighting a certain battle for 20 years. While driving down the road I told the Lord, "I am so sick and tired of this battle."

He asked, "Are you really tired of it?"

I said, "God, I am so tired of it."

And He said, "Then why don't you just tell it to be gone? Why don't you just cast it into the sea?"

I thought about it for a minute and thought, *Well, how does that even work?*

Then the Lord taught me about the kinds of mountains and their purposes. There are some mountains that are meant to be climbed. When Abraham went to the top of the mountain, it was to make a sacrifice (Genesis 22:1-18). It was to make a covenant with the Lord. And there are times when you're to go up that mountain.

There are times when you're going to go around a mountain to get to the other side. There are times you're going to go through a mountain to get to the other side—but there are also times when you need to tell that mountain to be gone, *be gone!*

BE GONE!

This particular mountain was a situation I had been dealing with for years. I dealt with it in every way I knew how. But it just wouldn't change. It was like I wasn't speaking the right language. I couldn't explain myself. It was so frustrating.

It wasn't anything bad, just frustrating. I was tired of dealing with the same frustration over and over and over. I remember driving down the road and I thought, *Okay, Lord, if it's that easy, then I'm going to do it.* So I spoke to that mountain and said, "I want you to be removed, and I do not want to deal with this mountain anymore, mountain be gone, be removed, be cast into the sea. This mindset is broken, it's gone, it's over." And I tell you the most wondrous thing happened, and it didn't even take a minute—immediately everything changed.

The whole narrative that I was battling in my mind and my spirit with another individual changed. I had been trying to work things out with someone, trying to explain myself but I couldn't communicate in a way the person could understand me correctly. It just was so frustrating. And then all of a sudden the frustration was gone.

It seemed the Lord was telling me, "Okay, you got it. Here's another piece of armor for you, another tool for your war chest." It was an amazing, amazing gift that God gave me. He gave me the ability to understand how I didn't have to go around that mountain again. He taught me what mountains to speak to, saying, "Be gone!"

Then God showed me the mountains I needed to climb to seek the face of God. Moses went to the top of the mountain to seek God's face (Exodus 3). You need to go to the top of the mountains to seek the Lord. You need to make your sacrifice there. You need to make your covenant there—it is a sacred place. What you get from God at the top of that mountain is what strengthens your walk in the valley, which will take you a long, long way. You have to have mountaintop experiences, or you're not going to make it through the valleys.

Jesus made it through the wilderness, the valleys, and to the mountaintops. He was not overcome by temptation (Matthew 4:1-11). He was not overcome by frustration. He was not overcome by the wear and tear of His physical body and His mind. He wasn't overcome by anything because He understood His mountains and His assignments on those mountains and how to accept them as God's will for Him.

I'm still working on learning my directions and trying not to get lost anymore. Yet, I am definitely reliant on the Holy Spirit in everything I do and everywhere I go. I can honestly say that none of those little experiences in my life have gone to waste in His Kingdom. The Lord has built upon them, precept upon precept, line upon line. And I am growing even to this day, and I'm in my mid-50s. I'm still growing and learning; and the more in tune I stay with the Holy Spirit, the more I grow.

Jesus wasn't overcome because He understood His mountains and His assignments.

The Holy Spirit is the greatest Navigator in your life. He will take you. He will show you. He will lead you. He will guide you. He's gracious, He's patient. He doesn't get frustrated. All of the frustrating situations that come into your life do not come from Him. But He is with you to handle each one.

The Bible says we can tell by the fruit that we bear if we are learning the lessons God teaches us (Matthew 7:16-23). If we're bearing the fruit of the Holy Spirit, our patience grows greater when we're dealing with people. We're more patient when we're dealing with frustrating situations. We mature, and we grow. And that's something I'm learning as I go along. My patience has become greater in so many areas.

I've also learned there are situations that you just don't need to even mess with. You don't even need to think about them. You have to have a quick answer to some situations and either avoid them or deal with them directly. That's a whole new way of being able to navigate. It's so important to know how to navigate. Navigation is not just going forward. Sometimes, you have to make hairy turns; sometimes, you have to go in reverse. Sometimes, you may have to go into a different lane, whatever it is, but you have to be confident in your navigation to go the way the Holy Spirit is leading you.

The Holy Spirit is the greatest navigator in the whole universe. As mentioned previously, you need to learn how to hear Him speak in the very small things like at the grocery store and hearing Him say, "Hey, you might want to pick up some milk." And you're thinking, *I just bought milk yesterday.* But you don't know that your neighbor is going to come over and ask for 2 cups of milk. The Holy Spirit knows you have to have the milk they need to borrow. You don't always know why He tells you to do something.

It's not about knowing why. It's about practicing your obedience.

If you can be obedient in small things, then when it comes to the big things in life that really can knock your feet out from beneath you, you have all of the small-thing experiences to draw from. You can stand strong when the world seems to be in turmoil. When nothing seems to be going right, when things seem to be so backward and crazy and you don't even know how to think about all of this, you will remain standing. When you don't know what's going to happen tomorrow, you have confidence in the Holy Spirit that He's going to lead you and guide you and that you will be fine.

Not only are you going to be fine, but your kids are going to be fine, and your grandkids are going to be fine because you have learned how to trust in the Lord. You can trust Him. He's not your copilot. He is your *Pilot!* You need to trust in all that He says and does, and you need to trust in His heart.

Let Him navigate your life. He has the plan and the purpose for your journey.

SECTION FIVE

What If I Don't Want To?

Kicking Against the Pricks

Jesus called out to them and said,

"Come and follow me, and I will transform you into

people who catch people for God."

Matthew 4:19 TPT

Then Jesus said to his disciples,

"If you truly want to follow me,

you should at once completely reject and disown your own life.

And you must be willing to share my cross and

experience it as your own,

as you continually surrender to my ways."

Matthew 16:24 TPT

12

Dream to Reality

Sometimes, I think I know what God is doing when He sends me out. But sometimes when I am obedient to His instructions, I see that He knows what I can't know, so He has a different reason than I understood.

One of those times was preceded by a dream God gave me. It was an impactful dream, but I didn't understand the meaning until much later.

In the dream, I was on a platform in front of a sea of beautiful women wearing colorful scarves on their heads; the scene was so lovely. However, it was a nightmare for me. I couldn't even imagine speaking in front of so many people. In the dream, I thought I was in Pakistan. When I told Troy about the dream, he said that I probably would not be going to Pakistan. Time passed, and the dream faded to the back of my memory.

One day, much later, we received an email. This was when home computers were coming into everyone's homes, and emails first came out. The email was from a young man, Alfred Mohanty. In the email, he told us about his dad who was a pastor. He asked us to pray for him and asked if we could meet him. His dad, Sadir Mohanty, was coming to the States. We said, sure, we would love to meet him. They didn't know the geography of America, but they thought he would be close to where we are. Come to find out, he was in Nashville, Tennessee. That year, we were home-schooling our kids, who were still really small. So we packed them up and drove to Nashville, Tennessee, to meet this pastor from India whom we had never met. His son talked so highly of him that we were very encouraged to go meet him.

When we first met him, he broke out his photo album of all of his ministry. We saw pictures of all that they were doing, including feeding children and people in the leper colonies. We absolutely love the people living in the leper colonies. The people are outcasts and have to live in walled cities and are not allowed to leave. Amazingly, we saw so much hope and so much faith in the lepers who live there. The Indian people believe that there are over three million gods. They are taught about all those gods from the time they are in preschool. Even the Christians are taught about these three million gods because that is their culture. They get to pick the ones they want to serve and worship.

The lepers know that all the other gods have forsaken them—all except Jesus. The lepers and their families live in a secluded place reminding me of what the Garden of Eden may have been like. It is extremely clean and very pristine, kept that way so as not to spread the disease. They love Jesus there. He is the only God they serve. It is a beautiful place, and I love to go to them.

While the pastor was showing us pictures of leper colonies and his ministry, he came to a picture of many beautiful women sitting together. I thought it was a large women's conference as thousands were sitting under a big awning. I looked closely at the picture and I realized that this was the vision God had given me in the dream. I had never considered India, I thought it was Pakistan because of the way the women were dressed. Much later, I had the opportunity to visit that area in India.

I went to India for the first time with our friend who is a very engaging person. I went to see the orphans and minister to them as part of the kids' crusades. When I arrived, I realized they thought I would be preaching like Troy does when he is there. Which meant they thought I was going to preach for four hours. They introduced me, and I spoke for a while; but I spoke just what I had on my heart to say. It certainly was not four hours.

I handed the program back over to the host, which was a little awkward. After they figured out that I wasn't a preacher, they took me to a gathering of a large group of women. There were only about six men, the rest were women. The women were all so beautifully dressed in colorful scarves.

One stood out to me like Esther did in her time. God highlighted her to me, saying, "That is what the woman at the well looked like." Rather than giving the message I had prepared, He gave me a message about the woman at the well, which is an incredible story about redemption and forgiveness and so many important truths that He wanted the women to know. Jesus reveals the true love of God through the story found in John 4:1-26.

In the Indian culture, men sit on one side of wherever they are, and women sit on the other. They don't intermingle. They still arrange marriages; the boys and girls don't have anything to do with each other until they get married. Everything that happened that day was contrary to my culture. I was a woman, and women can't be evangelists in that culture. I was a Christian and most Indians are Hindu, and yet the Lord had me deliver a message about Him and His love to these women. At that point, I didn't care what rules

I was breaking! I knew the Lord was working through me, and that surpassed everything else.

At the end of the message, massive numbers of women came to be saved and healed. Some of them were being set free from demonic oppression. It was a powerful, beautiful work of the Lord, and I was astounded that He had done that through me.

Then, I discovered just how astounding it was.

Later that evening, when we were driving home, Alfred was with us, and he asked me, "How did you know that those women were all prostitutes?" I'm sure the shocked look on my face gave credibility to my answer, "I didn't know they were."

He explained their culture and told me that it was a whole village of prostitutes. In India, the people are separated by sects. If they are the lower caste, they stay in one section. The higher caste people are in another area. All the prostitutes are in the same area. I had no idea; this was my first trip there. I learned that night about their culture and how it all worked. It is very different from our Western culture.

As Alfred was telling me about the prostitutes, I was shocked and in awe of God and His goodness. I didn't know, but He knew who my audience would be. He changed my sermon to speak to them. It touched their hearts in a powerful way. It touched me, too. It touched me to know He saw them and knew them and loved them enough to bring that word to them.

When I look back across my life, I see the fingerprints of God in everything. As I remember back to that time, I see His fingerprints, but I am also reminded of my mom and how God moved her to minister to those prostitutes' children. I can see the fingerprints of my mom and dad in my life, too. Our spiritual DNA is from our parents. I see it continuing—I see it in my kids, and now I see it in my grandkids. His goodness is for the generations.

REBIRTH

The Lord told me He had given me a voice for women. His work was not only to save them, but He wanted to rebirth them. He wanted to give them back the life He created for them that had been taken from them. I'll never forget that day. I was in a strange country, away from all that was comfortable for me. In that place, I didn't have Troy, my brother, or my own mother to fall back on. I had Jesus.

I went to that place because of the mission I knew He had created for me. He met me there, and I thought I would do His work with orphans. But He used that to teach me that I will always need to stay close to Him because I can't possibly know all that He knows.

He set me fully free to follow Him. Once I was free, He could use me to set women free so they could find their own voice. All because I let Him give me mine.

I continued to be used to minister to the people of India, and the following trip will always be especially meaningful to me.

We were in India on the east coast, and we went to a village church way up in the mountains. It was a very remote, poor village where the people lived on the side of a cliff. We had to climb up the mountain to get there. They mostly do everything at night because it is too hot in the daytime to do much of anything. The people were so poor they didn't have water or electricity in the village. To have church for us that night, they had to connect a cord to a power source at the bottom of the mountain and then connect additional cords to reach up to the village so there could be one light in the church. There were beautiful, caring people in this small church. They really loved Jesus and were so excited about having church that evening. The children all sat very nice and quiet. The women sat on one side, and the men sat on the other.

The Lord gave me my voice so He could use me to set women free to find their own voices.

I noticed one little boy who was about six years old. He could not sit still. He wasn't being unruly, but he was tapping other kids on the head and wiggling; he just couldn't sit still. Some of the adults tried to get him to be still. They tolerated him because they knew what was wrong with him. We didn't know yet.

When I met Joshua, I was told he was born blind, so he had been blind his entire life. They thought he also had mental challenges. He didn't know how to socialize with the other kids. We prayed for him that night and asked the Lord to heal him. We didn't see his healing that night.

For the next couple of years, we went to that village again and again, and we always asked for Joshua and prayed for him, always asking God to heal him. One reason we prayed for him was because he lived in a very dangerous situation—he was blind and lived on the side of a mountain. But of course, the main reason we prayed was because Joshua needed to be healed, to be whole as God intended. As he got older, he got more and more disruptive and was a lot for the people to handle.

One time when we went back and climbed to the top of the mountain and got to the little church, Joshua was nowhere to be found. I looked everywhere for him and couldn't find him. I was very concerned for him. I went to the pastor and asked him to ask the people where Joshua was. He came back and told me they said he was asleep, and the people didn't want to go get him. I told him I had come a long way and wanted to see Joshua.

The people reluctantly went and got Joshua and brought him to us. I was so happy to see him because I was worried that something had happened to him. When he arrived, the church service was starting and he did his typical Joshua thing, distracting everybody around him. The people were obviously exasperated that they had to go get him and bring him to the service.

My brother, Darrell, and my husband, Troy, were there. We all prayed for him again, this was the fourth time we prayed and believed God for his healing. I took him to Pastor Gene Izaguirre, because with him we have seen blind eyes healed in Africa, Mexico, and Nepal. He has an anointing for healing. I asked Pastor Gene to pray for my friend Joshua because I really wanted to see him be healed. I took him to Troy and to Darrell and asked them to pray for him. We all prayed for him because the Lord wants to heal him. Then I took him to Pastor Jim Maxwell (our pastor), and he prayed for him as well—then he took a picture of him to take it back to his church so they could all pray for him, too.

As always, there was only one dim light in the church; and as Pastor Maxwell used his phone to snap a picture of Joshua, the camera flashed, and Joshua's expression completely changed. He saw something for the first time. He just stood there with an odd look on his face. I asked the pastor to do that again because I thought Joshua had seen the flash. So he did it again, and Joshua seemed to be stunned. The pastor took a third picture and Joshua grinned from ear to ear. He grabbed the phone, brought it close to his face, and looked at it. Joshua could see!

God healed him on that trip. That was one of the most exciting, incredible miracles that I personally saw. We had prayed for that little boy and believed for him for three years. We saw him four times, but we also prayed for him even when we weren't there. He was the happiest little boy. God miraculously healed him that night.

It wasn't long after that healing when we talked to our friend, Pastor Sadir Mohanty. He told us that the little boy didn't have any mental challenges. Once he was healed, he became a perfect student and one of the best kids in the village.

Seeing that little boy healed and experiencing that miracle is one of my favorite lifetime memories.

SECTION SIX

My Joy Comes from the Lord!

I love each of you with the same love that the Father loves me.

You must continually let my love nourish your hearts.

If you keep my commands, you will live in my love,

just as I have kept my Father's commands,

for I continually live nourished and empowered by his love.

My purpose for telling you these things is so that

the joy that I experience will fill your hearts

with overflowing gladness!

John 15:9-11 TPT

13

Walking in Grace

I heard a good friend of mine teach at our leadership gathering for the OpenDoor leadership team. Ron Cantor was talking about grace and was teaching in a way I had not quite heard or understood before. It was a greater understanding of what grace is. We go from faith to faith and to glory to glory and from everlasting to everlasting. The Lord teaches us and builds upon new levels in our lives. To me, this was a new level of understanding of what grace is.

I had been understanding that grace was a God-given ability to overcome. God gives us grace to overcome any situation. Grace is an anointing to walk through whatever we are walking through. Without that grace, we are not going to make it through to the other side of different situations. I have walked in His grace all my life. God has given me the ability to walk through things that are hard, uncomfortable, and unpleasant.

Ron gave grace a different light and level, and it has transformed my life in an incredible way. I had not heard it explained this way before.

He taught that when God lifts grace from you, it is because He wants you to move, and you haven't moved. When he taught that, it was a time in my life when I was involved in the children's ministry, which I absolutely loved. I still love it. Children's ministry is my favorite, which is why I do SPARK Worldwide, something God gave me. At that point, I was doing children's church, the youth ministry, at our OpenDoor Church. The Lord was taking me out of that place and leading me into pastoral ministry. He was putting me in a leadership role that, frankly, I didn't want to be in. I didn't want to do it, and I didn't know how to do it.

God lifts grace from you because He wants you to move and you haven't moved.

God began to lift grace off me regarding children's ministry. What used to work didn't work anymore. I couldn't figure out what was going on because everything I had ever done and had been so successful with just wasn't working anymore. I kept praying and asking the Lord what was going on. I asked Him, "Why is this so hard now? Why are all these things that have been so great and so successful not working now?"

When Ron shared that message, he said, "The times in your life when God wants you to move and you don't want to move or you don't move, God will remove the grace He had always had on you that has allowed you to do what you have done. When that happens, it is definitely time for you to move."

So that was confirmation for me that God had removed the grace from me in that ministry. I never thought He would do that. I thought this is the place He has for me; this is what I'm good at, this is what I love—and no matter what, I will be able to do it.

The children of Israel went through this type of situation as well. The grace to live in Egypt was removed from them. And then God removed them from Egypt. Even in the wilderness, they sometimes wanted to go back to where they had been—where they were comfortable. But He had removed the grace for that place for them.

That is what God did for me. He removed the grace because He knew I wasn't going to move willingly on my own. I loved it, and I was comfortable in that place. So He removed the grace so I would move on. It wasn't that the Children's Ministry was a bad place or that He wanted me to have a higher assignment. It was that He had a new assignment for me, and I was not going willingly to that new assignment. After that teaching, I had a greater understanding. I transitioned into a leadership role in a greater way as a pastor.

Children's church and that ministry were my hiding places. I liked little kids, I understood kids, I could teach kids, and I could be around kids and do great. Adults weren't my favorite people to be around.

I had to work to submit my will to the Lord's will and say, "Okay, I'm willing to get with whatever program You have for me. You have my yes. Along with my yes, You have my obedience. I am going to follow through with this."

That was the beginning of the transition in my life that took me from the children's ministry to the pulpit ministry. That ultimately has brought me to where I am now. I am a pastor at our church and have been for a few years. I have also finished my doctorate degree in ministry and theology, which is another goal I never thought in 10 million years that I would ever accomplish. But it was all part of His plan, and I had no idea what His plan was.

It is so important that as you grow and learn, you let the Lord take you from faith to faith and glory to glory and everlasting to everlasting. That way you don't get stuck in one place because it's comfortable, or it's familiar, or you're good at it.

When the Lord tells you to move, you need to move. He has a plan, He knows the end, He knows the beginning. It is just like going to school; you start out in elementary, but you don't stay there, even though you're comfortable there. It feels scary to move on to junior high, but once there, you get your sea legs and start getting good at it. Then all of a sudden, you have to go to high school; and when you get really comfortable there, you go on to college, then the workplace.

Life is constantly changing. We tend to think that once we get to a certain plateau, we will stay there. That's not the way it is in life in general, and it is particularly not that way in ministry. We continue to grow and change. In the Scriptures, we see all the apostles go through changes while spreading the Gospel. They didn't stay the same but adapted to the circumstances.

As parents, we start out one way as young parents, but we change, grow, and mature according to the needs of the children and family and the lessons learned along the way. Understanding grace this way at a whole new level was definitely a teaching that came at the right moment to impact my life.

14

Connected by Grace

There have been times in my life when, if I had been more in tune with the Holy Spirit, I would have stopped or changed things more quickly. It took me having to deal with something or someone over and over to be able to say, "Okay, this doesn't work." Sometimes this happens in relationships with people you think are good Christian people. Once I understood the revelation of grace, I realized that just because something is good, doesn't mean it's from God.

The body of Christ is joined together like a jigsaw puzzle. Each piece (person) fits somewhere, but if in the wrong place, nothing fits together. So many times we try to force people into spaces because they seem to belong to the same picture, but they don't actually fit in that place.

The Bible says don't be unequally yoked (2 Corinthians 6:14). We take that to mean in marriage, which is very, very true. Anybody who has a successful marriage will tell you that is 100 percent accurate. I have been married more than 35 years now, and you have to be equally yoked to be able to make it.

For you to be successful and happy and to enjoy your marriage the way God intended, you have to be joined together. To go on with ministry and life and family and all the things God has given you, you have to be equally yoked. A lot of issues are hard enough to deal with without trying to go through them without being one with your spouse.

Unequally yoked also refers to being in alignment with ministry and in alignment in business and in friendships. You have to be equally yoked with people. It doesn't mean that you are always going to agree 100 percent on everything. How boring would life be if we all had the same opinions and the same views of things? After all, the Scripture says in Proverbs 27:17 that iron sharpens iron, which means that sometimes you are going to disagree, and sparks might fly, but it makes you stronger and forges something within you.

Sometimes, the Lord will remove the grace in a friendship because He doesn't want you connected in that place. It doesn't mean that the people are harmful or not good, it just means that the puzzle piece doesn't fit right there. You need to ask the Lord, "What piece fits here for me to connect with all You want me to put together?" I wish I had learned that when I was younger.

The Lord may remove grace in a friendship if He doesn't want you connected in that place.

I have sometimes developed relationships because I connected with people I wanted to help or because I wanted to be nice or good to them. It is not always the Lord saying that He wants me to do that. Sometimes it's just me going before the Lord saying, "This is a good idea." But God sees they are in a different place in their journey, so it's not His idea. I might have messed up because I wasn't listening to the Holy Spirit. It is so important for us to listen to the Holy Spirit when we are making decisions. We can be led by our grace and our peace that comes from Him to know what works and what doesn't work.

It is so important to know what grace is. Grace is a gift God gives us. It isn't that He is being mean to us or not giving us what we want or need—it's really the opposite. Grace is about Him giving us what we want and what we need. We just have to believe that He sees what we can't see. He knows what we can't know.

Parents are better at assessing the needs and wants of their children. When they ask for something that will harm them, the answer will be no. They may think their parents are being mean or punishing them, or that their parents don't love or care about them. That is not true.

Sometimes Christian adults act like children when He says no. They treat Him like He is a mean father. He is not; He is a good Father. He knows the beginning from the end, and He always has our best interests in mind when making decisions. He loves us enough to tell us no.

I am so very grateful that God has many times told me "No," because I look back and can see that what I wanted wasn't good for me. I'm so grateful that Jesus did not let me walk in those places, or see those sights, or hear that message. I thank Him that He didn't give me what I insisted on having. I had no idea that what I wanted would have turned my life upside down and inside out. I would have missed out on so many incredible opportunities by thinking that I knew better than He did. God always knows best.

Always remember that He knows all, and always believe and trust Him. His ways are higher than our ways; His thoughts are higher than our thoughts (Isaiah 55:9). He is a good Father, and He loves us. And sometimes good fathers spank their children. Sometimes when you are throwing a fit, trying to get your way, the Lord will say, "Okay, you need a time-out. You sit here for a few minutes and think about your behavior. I'm giving you time to reboot." That is His goodness toward us. It is not punishment. He doesn't punish us for His glory. He protects us, loves us, and brings us to the perfect place where He can fellowship with us, and we can be one with Him. He is the good Father—we have to remember that.

15

The Story of Grace

Grace is a young girl who is part of the Uganda family. We met her when she was 12, and she is now 23. She is a beautiful young girl. Grace was born with no legs and only one arm. She is one of the most amazing human beings I have ever met. Lisa and I have had the opportunity to spend months at a time with Grace. We like to say that there is nothing Grace can't do. She has made it through life, has made it through college, and has overcome every obstacle set before her. She even has a beautiful young son she named Shadrach because of the circumstances in which she became pregnant. She said she went through the fire, but she didn't come out smelling of smoke. I love her attitude about life. Her testimony is incredible.

Grace has an astounding ability to overcome obstacles while displaying gentle peace and true grace. She demonstrates how to keep going no matter what life throws at her. Lisa and I have taken her into the capital city of Uganda. As we walk around with her, people stare and talk about her, and are afraid of her because she looks different. She keeps her head up high as we go along. She prefers not to use a wheelchair, so she gets around with one hand by scooting herself along. It is really remarkable to see.

One day, Troy was really sick during the Covid mess. So I took him to the hospital because he thought he was having a gallbladder attack. They did a bunch of X-rays, ran some tests, and gave him some medicine. I wasn't allowed to go in, so I waited in the car for a couple of hours. They called in a prescription to the pharmacy, and he was told to pick up a few things from the grocery store and to call a surgeon to schedule a time to have his gallbladder removed.

The hospital was about 45 minutes from our house. As we were driving home, he was feeling worse and worse. He looked terrible. When we got to the pharmacy for his prescription, it wasn't ready yet. Our small grocery store is about three miles from the pharmacy. I told Troy to drop me off at the grocery store so I could get what we needed. He could return to the pharmacy and drive through to pick up the medicine while I shopped, then he could come back and get me. I had driven him to the hospital in my car because he was feeling so sick.

I was in the grocery store, my cart was full, and I was ready to check out when Troy called. He asked where my car key was. He had decided to park and go into the pharmacy to get the medicine. He never ever goes into the pharmacy, he just goes through the drive-through. I was a little agitated. Our car has a push start/ stop and it won't start unless it detects a key fob, which I had in my purse. There was no way for me to get from the grocery store to the pharmacy without walking down a major highway. So all this stuff is going on in my head, and I'm having an argument with him. Of course, it's only in my head, not out-loud real.

I told the store clerk I had to leave my grocery cart and promised I'd be back after I took the car key to my husband so I could start my car. So I start walking alongside the main highway. I'm frustrated and angry because I'm sure he's upset at me for not leaving the key in the car for him. I'm going over the whole thing in my head while walking along a busy road to the pharmacy. Then the Lord reminded me, "You have legs."

And I said, "I do have legs."

He said, "Grace walks that far every day with one hand, she has no legs, and she does not complain like you are."

I felt the conviction of the Lord like I had never felt before. And I thought, *That's so bad of me. I should be grateful I have legs. I travel all around the world and see how far people have to walk. I see all the conditions they have to walk through—the jungles, the mud and dirt. They have to walk through dangerous places. I have a straight, relatively safe walk, yet I'm so mad that I have to hike a few miles to aid my sick husband. I'm being ridiculous.*

In that moment the Lord spoke to me again about grace. Not Grace the girl, but about the grace I needed to have in life for other people. And to see that when He has called me to do something, I need to look at it in the right way, with the right perspective. I need to see it from His point of view. I need to look at what I *do have* instead of what I don't have and be grateful for everything I have.

I told Grace that story, and then I said, "You know what? You teach me so many life lessons through your outlook, attitude, your love and grace. You will never know how many life lessons you have taught me. Thank you, dear friend." I'm sure I'm not the only one she has taught and influenced over the years. Just because she was born different doesn't mean she doesn't have a testimony and a story from which we can all learn—in fact her physical appearance evokes inspiration, courage, and stamina that has no doubt touched countless people's hearts.

I need to look at what I have, not at what I don't have, and be grateful for everything I have.

We are all different, none of us are alike. We all have our own special giftings and talents and quirks. We need to be thankful for what God has given us. We need to remember His blessings. Our attitude and our heart are dependent on us having the right mind. When the Lord showed me that, it changed my heart and changed my mind.

When I walked into the pharmacy parking lot, I wasn't mad at Troy. And of course, he wasn't mad at me. He was just sick and wanted to go home. I have never responded to a situation in that frame of mind ever again. And I remember to take my key out of my purse when I get out of my car.

And I remember Grace.

Created in His Image

*Be Yourself,
Everyone Else Is Taken*

For you have acquired new creation life

which is continually being renewed

into the likeness of the One who created you;

giving you the full revelation of God.

In this new creation life,

your nationality makes no difference,

nor your ethnicity, education, nor economic status—

they matter nothing.

For it is Christ that means everything as

he lives in every one of us!

Colossians 3:10-11 TPT

16

Time Travel and Being Poor

People like to imagine what it would be like to travel through time. Someone asked me, "If you could go back in time, what would you tell yourself back then because of things you now know?"

It was more like the Lord did a reverse time travel with me. He would tell me things when I was in the midst of something that was hard. He would say to me, "It's not going to be like this in the future. This is what it is going to be like." Then He would show me what I didn't understand at the time.

In the midst of being poor, He would say, "You're not always going to be poor. It is going to look like this," and then He showed me how it would be. I couldn't visualize it or understand it because I had always been poor. I knew what poor was like, and I was actually good at it. I could do poor, really well. I would ask Him what it would look like, and I couldn't grasp it at that point in time. But now I'm living it, and there are times I remember those conversations with Him. It was His way of preparing me for where I am now. I'm not poor anymore, and I don't have a poverty mindset anymore.

Poverty is not just a financial state. It is a mindset, and it is a spirit of not having enough. My whole life, I have always had enough. I might not have had more than enough, but I have had enough.

The Lord showed me that the day would come when I would have an abundance. He said that I was solid in that place of poverty, and it wasn't going to mess me up in that place of abundance. I heard T.D. Jakes preach on the Scripture that says God won't put more on you than you can handle (1 Corinthians 10:13). Most think that verse means God will not allow the terrible things that happen in our lives to break us. But sometimes, God says you can't handle the blessings He has for us.

God is not going to put a blessing on you if you aren't ready for it. He doesn't release it to us because it will ruin us. For example, look how many people are ruined by success—lottery winners, for example. God says, "I'm not going to let you get ruined by success. I am keeping you in this holding pattern for as long as I have to so you won't be ruined. If I give it to you before you are ready, it will destroy you, and I love you too much for that."

> ## God won't release a blessing in our life if we aren't ready for it. It would ruin us.

It was in that place when God said, "You are going to be success-ful, and it will not ruin you. You are already satisfied here in this place. But the things you are going to do will blow your mind." That is so true today. What we get to do blows my mind. I'm so grateful for the doors God has opened for us.

I never thought I would be successful. I knew Troy would be, but I never thought about it for me. When God gave me my ministry, I had never even had a vision of it, I was surprised by my calling. To me, my ministry was to be a mom and a wife. It is still my priority to be a mom and a wife. To me, success is having good kids and a happy husband who can do all that he needs to do. So, I have always felt successful. But as the world sees success, I never saw myself as that. I have always been so satisfied in who I am and what I get to do to serve the Lord and His children.

17

Take Him at His Word

Several years ago, my brother, Darrell Knight, started working with me at SPARK Worldwide. It is a great venture because as teenagers, we had decided to do ministry together. We were going to "do missions" (spread the Gospel near and far) and make a difference in the world. Life happened, and he wound up getting married and becoming an extremely successful businessman in his photography ventures. He was doing all the things God had put in his heart to do.

I went into ministry with my husband, Troy, and we started doing missions and all the things God put into my heart to do. It was all beautiful and amazing.

Then Darrell told me he really believed he had heard God speak to him, telling him to retire and work for me. It made me so happy because it reminded me of the promise God gave us as kids that we would one day work together. We knew we would do missions together and ministry together, so it was so exciting to have this happen.

But our working relationship came with challenges, not so much for me but for him. He was a very successful businessman, and I was a very successful ministry leader. We had a large church and several ministries outside of our church, so I understood how business works. But I also understood how faith and hope work together in ministry.

My brother came to work with me as a businessman with a business mindset, not a ministry mindset. He told me we needed to sit down together so I could explain his responsibilities, as he was going to take over the operations of SPARK for me. I loved being the one who cast the vision, but he was going to be the one who carried it out. He wanted to map out the business plan.

I remember sitting across from him thinking, *What the heck is a business plan?* It was so funny to see the sheer look of terror on his face when I asked him, "What do you mean by a business plan?"

He said, "Okay, let's just start with this: What are your goals for the next five years?"

I told him that right now I was feeding 500 kids a month and wanted to feed 5,000 kids a month by the end of the next year. He said that was a good plan. I went on and told him about the outreach I wanted to do, and what I wanted to do for the local kids, and all the great plans I had.

He said, "Those are all great goals. How are we going to accomplish this, Leanna? How do you raise money? How do you get the funds to do these things?"

I told him we held an Annual SPARK Gala to make people aware of what we do. At that time, we didn't have a very big platform, so I didn't have very many people to share it with, but I shared it with anyone who would listen.

He looked at me and asked again, "How do you expect this to happen, Leanna?" Then he said we had to have an actual business plan and would have to change some things.

I told Darrell that, I knew that it would all work out, it always did. And that God had told me He wanted me to increase from here to there, so by faith I knew it would happen. I don't know if he looked at me with horror, fear, terror, or what that look was, but I translated it as, *Is she kidding, or is she being serious?*

HOPE IS A BUSINESS PLAN?

When he realized I was serious, he said, "Leanna, hope is not a business plan."

I just laughed and told him, "Actually, it is, and it has worked really well for me."

He said it was great that it had worked up until now, but I wouldn't be able to increase and do all that I wanted to do if I just had hope as a business plan. He said I had to have strategies and ways of figuring it all out to reach the goals I set for the ministry.

I sat and pondered what he said. Then I told him that was why God sent him to work with me. I was going to continue on this lovely path of believing that if God says it, He will do it. I will continue to partner with Him in everything He says for me to do, and I believe Him when He tells me I can do it.

Fast-forward, and now, years later, my brother believes in hope as a business plan even more than I have hope as a business plan. His expectations of God showing up and doing are so much greater than they were; they have increased. Now he has hope as his business plan.

Hope isn't wishing. Hope is believing what God has said He is going to do. Hope is having faith that God is as good as He says He is. Hope is putting action to what you believe God is saying.

Hope is believing what God has said He is going to do.

Hope isn't just sitting back and waiting for something "magical" to happen. You have to put action to your faith. You have to walk it out. You have to ask the hard questions, "If I am going to increase to feeding 5,000 children from 500 children, I have to increase my ability to get people to sponsor these children. How am I going to do that?" We decided to take more people with us on mission trips so they can catch the vision. And that has worked for us.

GOD WORKING THROUGH YOU

A calling is different for everybody, depending on how God speaks to you and how He deals with you. It depends on what He is saying to you and what He wants to do through you. That was one of the many cases where God showed us how He was working through us. He is very personal, and He is very unique because your ministry is going to be unique in all that He has for you and how He deals with you as a person. He is not going to deal with you the same way He deals with everyone else. He is not a corporate God; He is a personal God.

One time when we were in Mexico, we met a little boy named Luis. I have a heart not for the "bad" little boys but for the tenacious ones. They are a little more strong-willed and a little more testing. I love those who believe and have the courage to push the envelope. They have the strength and the courage to say, "I can do this." I love to see that character trait in people. Luis was one of those little guys.

Luis has a very rare skin disease. His poor little face looked like wrinkled leather. He is a sweet boy and smart as a whip. But that little boy was a turkey. He was always in trouble because he pushed the envelope to see how far he could go. I loved that about him.

We had gone to Mexico on a mission trip. Darrell and my sister-in-law, Mendy, were with me. We had been asked to take care of kids in an orphanage who were Tarahumara Indians, indigenous to Mexico and beautiful, small-statured people. When we arrived, we were told the plight of these 50-plus kids. The man who had been taking care of them had died and the children were taking care of each other. Consequently, we spent time cleaning out the place and restoring order. Darrell, Mendy, and their small children spent time working in the facility to make it better for the kids and establish orderliness.

We witnessed incredible acts of redemption during our time at that orphanage. Troy and I had the privilege of being there with our small kids every other weekend, and we poured lots of love into those kids and blessed them with food and supplies and helped them in various ways.

Because they had been in this facility for a very long time, all alone, taking care of each other, almost starving to death, we decided to take them to the closest town and have a pizza party. They probably had never experienced anything like that. So we decided to have a party for them.

We arranged for a bus and took about 60 kids to town. After eating pizza, we walked over to the town square where there was a really neat, old-school candy shop. Darrell and Troy were explaining to the kids that when they went into the candy shop, they could have anything they wanted. It was a bakery as well as a candy store. As Troy was talking to them, he told them he had a credit card, so they could have anything they wanted. Of course, they didn't have any idea what a credit card was.

They went into the store and looked around at all the goodies. Then each kid brought to Troy one small piece of candy, just one little piece. A tootsie roll, a gum drop, or whatever. Troy told them they could have as many as they wanted of whatever they wanted. So they went back and got one more little piece of candy. They just didn't understand—they never had that kind of freedom of choice.

Meanwhile, Darrell was managing the children between the store and the bus, and Troy was inside. And Mendy and I were just having fun watching all these kids get to live their best lives.

LUIS BELIEVED

When it was time to go, Troy paid for the candy, and we all boarded the bus. Except Luis. We found him back in the store. "Okay, Luis, it's time to go," we called as we saw him at the back of the store. When we were close enough to hear, he was telling the people working there that he wanted the big, three-tiered wedding cake. They were looking at him like he was crazy and telling him no. But he was telling them yes.

Luis believed. He believed what he was told—that he could have anything he wanted. And you know what? He came walking out of that shop with that wedding cake. The kids were hanging out the bus windows saying, "Oh, Luis, you're going to be in big trouble." He was just smiling, carrying his cake that was almost bigger than him, and he got on the bus. The kids were used to him being in trouble and were taunting him. But Luis just looked at them and said, "The gringo said we could have whatever we want."

That whole scenario was such a faith builder for me, Troy, and our whole team. Whatever God says, He means it. You just have to believe it! Luis believed it.

Luis didn't get the cake just for himself. As soon as he was settled on the bus, he shared the cake with all the kids. When you believe what God says, and you take Him at His word, it isn't just for you, it's for everyone around you, too.

That was one of the many life lessons God has given me through the ministry of reaching out and transforming lives. I can be the hands, feet, and heart of Jesus to kids and people everywhere because I believe Him. You too can trust what He says, and you can have as much of Him as you want.

I have seen God show up in big ways when He has given us big projects. He is the One I seek in order to know what the ministry is to do. When I hear Him, I believe Him. When I believe Him, I step out in faith and obey Him and act on what He says to do.

At Christmas for the past 30 years, we distribute 3,000 backpacks full of brand-new toys for every age group, from babies all the way to 18 years old. We do a huge outreach on the border of Matamoros, Mexico, and Brownsville, Texas—and it's a big deal to us, it is important. After we give out the backpacks, we have a big party in the neighborhood near Mission Divina, the church we partner with there.

We also take care of local kids here. For the local kids, we sponsor what started off as 150 kids, and has now grown to between 500 to 600 kids. One particular year, we were providing gifts and food for about 300 kids—we were taking care of their entire Christmas. Otherwise, these kids would have received nothing. As always, when we decide to take on an outreach, we do it all the way, we represent King Jesus the very best we can.

We shop individually for the children and spend around $200 to $300 on each. The parents give us a list with the gifts their kids really want. They also give us a list of what the big kids need. Maybe $200-$300 doesn't seem like a lot, but this particular Christmas time it was. We were having a really hard time with funding the outreach; we just didn't have the financial resources.

It was coming down to crunch time, and we had only shopped for about half our kids. We needed a very large amount of money—several hundred thousand dollars—to come in to finish both projects. I woke up one morning saying, "Okay, God, today is the last day we have to get all of the outreach projects finished, and there is no money. There is no money. I know there is going to be, so I am saying yes. I am sending my teams out, and we are going to find all the gifts, toys, and clothes we need to give to the children. I am believing that the money is going to be there."

The next morning, Darrell and Lisa, my very good friend and partner, and my daughter-in-law, Brandi who helps me shop, were getting ready to go shopping. Before we left, Darrell went to the mailbox. We don't receive very much mail anymore because most of our funds come in electronically or people drop off a check. He came back and said, "You aren't going to believe this. Somebody sent us a ten thousand dollar check!" We were all so excited and started thanking the Lord.

Then Lisa, who takes care of our finances, looked at the check more closely. She said, "This isn't a 10 thousand dollar check—it's a *100 thousand dollar check!*"

God had given us the $100,000 that we needed to finish what we had started. He always finishes what He starts. He always does it better than what we can hope or even imagine (Ephesians 3:20). We have to believe Him. We have to trust Him. We have to hear Him and know that what He says is true.

That is the goodness of God in the land of the living.

SECTION EIGHT

And Now...

Jesus says, "There is so much more I would like to say to you,

but it's more than you can grasp at this moment.

But when the truth-giving Spirit comes,

he will unveil the reality of every truth within you.

He won't speak on his own,

but only what he hears from the Father,

and he will reveal prophetically to you what is to come.

He will glorify me on the earth,

for he will receive from

me what is mine and

reveal it to you."

John 16:12-14 TPT

18

Keys That Open Doors

Our ministry, OpenDoor Church, will soon be 29 years old. It has been such an amazing journey that God set us on all those years ago. Even though, when Troy proposed I made him promise he would not be a preacher. He said, "No way, that's never going to happen!" I said, "Okay, I will marry you."

It wasn't that I had bad experiences with church when I was growing up because I didn't. In the past, however, all I had seen was that a good pastor's wife could sing and play the piano. I couldn't do either of those, so I had decided that I was not good pastor's wife material. I couldn't see that working for me, and it wouldn't work for Troy if he became a preacher, so we got that out of the way. I also didn't want preachers' kids. I was friends with preachers' kids, and they were bad. I didn't want to raise bad kids.

I share all that with you because I can be honest with God. God knows what we're thinking, so we can just say (or write in this case) what's in our minds. It's not going to offend Him or shock Him. So, that was my stipulation saying yes to Troy's marriage proposal. He said he was a musician and was never gonna be a preacher. That was good enough for me. But Jehovah Sneaky didn't just make *him* a preacher, He made *me* a preacher, too. I thought, *Lord, what were*

You thinking? Yet I knew that His ways are higher than ours, and His thoughts are greater than ours.

In the beginning, Troy indeed was a musician who traveled all over "preaching" the Gospel through his music in places where "normal" Christians wouldn't go. Churchy Christians like me would never go into those places. Troy would remind me, "Leanna, the Lord sent us into all the world." But I would tell him, not into those bad places. But he knew that was where the people who needed to hear about the Lord would be. This was a real culture shock to me.

I was a church lady. I understood church, and church was my life. Yet, Troy would minister to the most unlikely people in places other than church. Next, we were reaching out to the homeless, which I didn't consider a bad place. Then we did street ministry. Then we started ministering to elderly shut-ins.

NO THANK YOU

And then one day, God called us to do our own ministry. We both said, "No thank You, You can pass that on to someone else. That's not what we do." Can you imagine our arrogance telling God, "No thank You"? We were young at the time. We thought we were smarter than our parents, and we thought we were smarter than God, too. We also thought we could negotiate with God. We told God that His offer was just probably not for us. We told Him that He could find somebody who does the church thing.

We said, "Lord, You need people who are smarter. He's a musician, and I'm a hairdresser, and this life is working great for us." He showed us that those two aspects of our lives were preparing us for this assignment. He showed us he gave Troy a talent and a gift to reach people, to entertain people, and to engage people. He gave him the gift of being a storyteller to draw people in. Then God show us that He gave me the ability to sit and listen and to make things beautiful and make people feel beautiful. He used those God-given gifts of ours to start the church. When God did indeed call us to start the church, and we knew it was Him, our answer was yes. There is no other answer when you are hearing from and talking to the Lord.

We told God that we would do this until somebody smart came along. We prayed about it and sought Him for direction. We told Him that we didn't even know how to start a church.

Everything we have ever done in our lives, at first we had no idea how to do it. There was no book and no one to tell us. So we just dove in and if it worked, great! If it didn't, we did something else. The Lord gave us that confidence. He is personal. He wants us to be dependent on the Holy Spirit and on Him. When we seek Him, and pray, He opens doors to opportunities and blessing galore.

OPEN DOOR

At that time, we didn't even know what to call the church. Then God gave Troy the name "OpenDoor," so we called it OpenDoor Fellowship, The Mission That Makes a Difference. We loved missions, and we were going to keep missions as a focus. We asked God, "Why can't we just be missionaries?" I'm telling you, don't challenge Him, just go with it. It's so much easier to do that. It is a quicker process to get where He wants you to be.

The Scripture God gave Troy was Revelation 3:7-9 (NKJV):

*And to the angel of the church in Philadelphia write, "These things says He who is holy, He who is true, 'He who has the key of David, He who opens and no one shuts, and shuts and no one opens': I know your works. See, **I have set before you an open door, and no one can shut it; for you have a little strength, have kept My word, and have not denied My name.** Indeed I will make those of the synagogue of Satan, who say they are Jews and are not, but lie—indeed I will make them come and worship before your feet, and to know that I have loved you."*

There is so much truth in that Scripture. We knew when the Lord told us "OpenDoor," and then He brought us to that Scripture that the church was going to be named OpenDoor, and we were to be the church of Philadelphia, which is the church of brotherly love. Pastor Troy, as the architect of the culture of this church, has kept true to the word that was given to him. He has kept it relational. It is so important to us that we maintain very relational, close ties with people.

We also find this in that passage of Scripture. He says, *"You have a little strength, but you have kept My word and have not denied My name."* You don't have to have it figured out. You don't have to be the smartest person in your class. You don't have to be the richest person on the planet. You don't have to be any of what the world tells you to be to do what God has called you to do. You don't have to be financially successful.

So many people say, "When I have enough money I will start a family." You're never going to have enough money to start a family. You're never going to have children if you believe that money is the key to family life. Some people say that when they get enough money, they will tithe. That is never going to happen either. The "more" you are chasing is never going to be enough; it's never going to happen.

But to this church and to you, God says, "You didn't have strength, didn't have it figured out, didn't have the manpower, and didn't have any of the stuff that you thought you needed to do My will. Even so, you were faithful, and you believed Me." Then He says, "Because of that, I will open doors that nobody can open, and shut doors that nobody else can shut."

I live an hour away from the church, and while driving I love to listen to soaking CDs (soothing Christian music). So I was flipping through the radio stations, trying to find another station that would have that kind of music. A country song came on, and the words were, "Thank God for unanswered prayers." At first I thought it was kind of catchy, but then my reaction was no, that's not right. God always answers prayers. Sometimes, His answer is no. He may say, no, don't do that, or no, you can't have that. You may not like His answer, but I promise that you're going to look back some day and thank Him for His no because you'll be looking at a train wreck and glad you didn't have to go through that.

This Scripture in Revelation 3 says that the One who is true has the key of David, and He opens a door that no one can shut. The Lord is the only One who can open the door for you, and He is the only One who can shut the door. But there is a key to those doors, and He has been talking to me about keys.

KEYS

Keys represent authority and access. If I had a Porsche and I gave you my key, I would have given you the authority that belonged to me to drive it, and the key would give you access to it. The key would open the door that nobody else could open. I would have shown you that I trust you to drive my car. I opened the door for you to use the car, and nobody else can close it because you have the key.

The Lord does that. He gives you a key that will open a door that nobody else can close. But you have to use the key, you have to put it in the lock and unlock the door. Otherwise, it remains in your pocket, and you sit there whining and complaining. You are saying, "God, You have not answered my prayers. I've asked You, and You won't do this."

Yet God is saying, "You have the key to this answer; it is in your pocket."

I started asking the Lord what the Key of David was. Pastor Troy is a musician, and musicians understand the Key of David. It is the musical key musicians tune their instruments to. It's the sound of Heaven, the key of the sound of Heaven.

But I want you to think about keys that unlock doors. The key that Revelation is talking about is the anointing that David walked in. All of us have an anointing that we walk in. You can call it your superpower; you can call it whatever you want to. Your anointing is the gifting within your life that seems normal to you. It is where you think, *I'm good at that.* When other people make a big deal out of your anointing, you tell them it's not a big deal because it doesn't seem that way to you. You have a gifting that God put on your life specifically for you.

You have a gifting that God put on your life specifically for you.

It took me a long time to realize that my gifting is being a mom. God made me a mom. It's not because I have children that made me a mom. I have an *anointing* to be a mom. There's an anointing to be a father, teacher, carpenter, baker, whatever God chose for you. And there's a key to your anointing giving only you access to places where He wants You to go. You have the key in your hand; you have to use that tool to unlock your anointing.

The Scripture says to the church at Philadelphia, "You were faithful when you were weak." When you are faithful with that key, you get another key, then you get another key, and pretty soon you're like the janitor with a whole ring of keys. You will get to the place where you will have a key to every door there is. Then you can get in anywhere you need to be. But remember, the janitor is a servant. The more you serve, the more faithful you are, the more people will look at you as faithful and know they can trust you with more.

The Lord does the same with us. He looks at you and thinks, *I gave you this key, and you were so faithful. I can trust you.* When He can trust you, He knows He can give you more access to more opportunities to do His will.

Over our many years of ministry, we have visited numerous countries and cities worldwide. Many times the mayor of a city has given us the "key" to their city. I didn't know what to do with these very large but mostly meaningless keys. One day the Lord told me that these keys meant we were being given access to that area. The people were saying they trusted us and were giving us authority in that place. After that, those keys meant a great deal to me. I said, "Thank You, Lord, that other people see me different from how I see me."

People see us different from how we see ourselves. True friends and mentors will tell you the truth about yourself if you ask them. Let them tell you what they see in you. When you do that, you will discover gifts and talents and keys that have been in your pocket that you didn't know you had.

People have pulled things out of me that I had no idea were in me. I have learned in my years of faithfulness that in those times when I had nothing, I could trust the people God sent to be around me.

When He is the One who truly sends people to be part of your life, you can trust what they say they see in you. It may be that you don't see the person they see. If more than one person sees the same anointing, then you should start believing that you are who God says you are. You have the Key of David to go open these doors that no one can shut because God is opening them.

Someone could be a billionaire and still not have favor in their life like Pastor Troy and I do. A billionaire wouldn't get to do the things we do, or meet the people we meet, or have the opportunities we have to see lives transformed. Money doesn't provide those kind of opportunities—only the favor of the Lord blesses in that way. Favor is so much greater than any amount of money. There's nothing wrong with money; it helps people be able to do what God wants to be done. We have to have money to take care of all of the people who have needs. But that's not our goal. Our goal as believers is to have the favor of the Lord on our life. When we have His favor, we have access to all that the Kingdom of God contains.

In the sixteenth chapter of Matthew, Jesus was talking to His disciples at Caesarea Philippi. He asked them what people were saying about Him; He wanted to know who people said He was. His disciples told Him that some said John the Baptist, some said Elijah, some said Jeremiah, or other prophets.

> He said to them, "But who do you say that I am?"
>
> "Simon Peter answered and said, "You are the Christ, the Son of the living God."
>
> Jesus answered and said to him, "Blessed are you, Simon Bar-Jonah, for flesh and blood has not revealed this to you, but My Father who is in heaven. And I also say to you that you are Peter, and on this rock I will build My church, and the gates of Hades shall not prevail against it. And **I will give you the keys** of the kingdom of heaven, and whatever you bind on earth will be bound in heaven, and whatever you loose on earth will be loosed in heaven."
>
> Then He commanded His disciples that they should tell no one that He was Jesus the Christ (Matthew 16:15-20 NKJV).

If you have an encounter with Jesus, the Father is the One who has revealed Him to you. No one can reveal Jesus to you in a way that you have a close, intimate encounter with Him. Only the Father reveals Him to you.

When you encounter Jesus, it doesn't matter what you're going through or what hell is trying to throw at you—nothing can prevail against you. Jesus says that evil cannot prevail against you: "...*upon this rock I will build my church, and all the powers of hell will not conquer it"* (Matthew 16:18 NLT).

Do not let yourself get into that place of depression, anxiety, or the attitude that things are never going to get better. None of that thinking is real or true; it will pass! Your current challenge will be like a chapter in a book. It may be the most miserable chapter in the whole book. But turn to Jesus and then the next chapter is rainbows and butterflies and wonders of the Kingdom. You have to trust the Lord that hell cannot prevail against you, cannot conquer you. That's what the Word says.

Jesus says that He will give you the keys of the Kingdom of Heaven, and whatever you bind on earth will be bound in Heaven, and whatever you loose on earth will be loosed in Heaven.

PRAY AND OBEY

He then tells His disciples not to tell other people He is Jesus, the Christ. That seems odd, but it is really insightful. There will be intimate moments between you and Jesus when He will give you keys that are just between you and Him. You have to be intimate with Jesus to hear Him speak and to hear the Father speak.

Maybe you have had a "What Would Jesus Do" bracelet? The answer: Jesus would pray. Often Jesus said He had to get away and hear the Father speak (see Luke 5:16; Matthew 26:36,42; Mark 1:35 and others). He would get away to hear what the Father said, then He would do what the Father told Him. He would say what the Father said. He didn't do whatever He felt like doing. He didn't do whatever emotion was telling Him or what someone else said He needed to do. He prayed and obeyed.

Jesus got in trouble when He didn't join the family to travel home from Jerusalem. His mother said, *"Son, why have You done this to us? Look, Your father and I have sought You anxiously"* (Luke 2:48 NKJV). His heavenly Father told Him that He was to obey His mama. Luke 2:51-52 records for us that, *"Then He went down with them and came to Nazareth, and was subject to them, but His mother kept all these things in her heart. And Jesus increased in wisdom and stature, and in favor with God and men."* So Jesus understood that His mother had authority over Him. He was a quick learner.

So years later, I believe that when Jesus's mother told Him to do something at a wedding, there is an important teaching for us to understand (John 2:1-11). When His mother learned there was no more wine to serve the guests, she told Jesus He had to do something. Jesus replied that it wasn't His time yet. The Bible doesn't give us the whole picture, but I think He went and talked to His heavenly Father about what His mother said to Him.

I think He went to the Father and said His mom told Him to do something. Then maybe Jesus said something such as, "I'm supposed to do what You say I'm supposed to do, Father, and You have not told me anything about this situation. This will be a miracle, and You haven't told Me to start doing miracles yet."

I think His Father told Him to mind His mama and everything would work out. So Jesus told the servants to fill the water pots with water—that turned into even better wine than was first served.

The Bible doesn't tell every detail, but we can get insight from the fact that Jesus said, "I only do what the Father tells me to do" (John 5:19).

You don't need to do anything until you go to the Father to seek His voice about the matter. There are life decisions that you will have to make. First, you need to hear the Father speak. You need to do what He tells you. If you do that, you will make the right decision. You can't lose if you do what He tells you to do.

Jesus went to hell and said in essence, "Too bad, devil, I am here to take away the keys. You no longer have power and authority over My people." Jesus's sacrifice on the Cross means that the devil no longer has power or authority over us.

Jesus has the keys, and He is giving them to us and telling us to choose life. He came to give us life, and life more abundant than we have ever known. In Matthew 18:19-20 (NKJV), Jesus says:

> *Again I say to you that if two of you agree on earth concerning anything that they ask, it will be done for them by My Father in heaven. For where two or three are gathered together in My name, I am there in the midst of them.*

Jesus is saying that if you are gathered in His name, He has given you His keys and His authority, and if you come together in unity, there is nothing you can't do. Pastor Troy and I have seen that truth come to life. When we are in unity, when we agree, we come before the Father because we know His heart. He has told us to do some of the most impossible, incredible things that neither of us had a skill set for, we didn't have an answer for, and we weren't prepared for—but we know we heard Him speak so we prayed and obeyed.

And look at what has happened because we have! In 29 years, we are a church that is impacting the world for Jesus, and we've set captives free with the keys He has given us. We are like the old-school jailer with the big ring of keys—we walk in and set people free. When Pastor Troy goes in to rescue kids, he says, "I have the key that is going to set you free." He takes the authority that Jesus gave him and sets people free from all types of bondage.

I am anointed to go in as mom to all the kids and make sure they have a family. I make sure they are taken care of in all the ways they need. Walking in that anointing brings me joy!

Walking in your anointing is life giving. If you are feeling exhausted and miserable, ask God where your key is. Seek Him and ask Him to show you where your key is. You have to find your key because you can't walk in someone else's anointing. You need the key He has for you to walk in because it will open the door to your perfect place in the body of Christ. We are all part of His body, and there is a perfect place where you fit. Ask the Lord where your key is. Get that one key from Him, walk in that, and soon He will give you another key.

Jesus entrusts us with the keys to His Kingdom so we can share the Gospel, so we can renew our minds, so we can enjoy life abundantly, and so we can have intimacy with the Lord. Jesus opened the door to our salvation as only He could. He has so much more in the Kingdom for each of us. Let Him open those doors for you, too.

19

Seasons

Recently God told me to study the seasons. I wasn't sure what that meant, but that was clearly what He said. I knew He was changing my seasons—letting me know something was going to be different. At this point I'm not sure what different means but I do know that I should expect a new season and that it's going to be good.

God told me that seasons are like chapters in a book. Whenever He takes us into a new season, the old season is finished. That chapter is closed, and the new chapter looks nothing like the last chapter.

I believe God is telling me that the coming season is going to look wildly different—not just for me but for the entire body of Christ. I am super excited about what He is going to do and what He is doing.

He also reminded me that I can't go on to the next chapter of life if I keep reading the last chapter over and over. You have to go from old to new, from the old wineskin to the new wineskin, because He is doing a new thing. He says in Scripture, *"For I am about to do something new. See, I have already begun! Do you not see it?"* (Isaiah 43:19 NLT).

You can't go to the next chapter of your life if you keep reading the last chapter.

I believe He is saying during this whole time of navigation of positioning yourself for promotion from the field to the palace, you are to be looking for and seeing what He is doing in your life. You need to be extremely intentional about hearing His voice.

20

And Now

I am currently 55 years old and about to have a birthday. I am graduating with my Doctorate Degree in Ministry and Theology in a week. That is an act of obedience to follow what God said to me about going to school many years ago. I started out in one career and finished in another because He changed my course. I always have a yes for Him. I don't always have it figured out when I say yes, but I do have this figured out—when He changes my direction, I have to change accordingly.

It isn't that He has changed His mind (James 1:17; Hebrews 6:17, 13:8)—it's that I'm catching up with what He already had planned for me. A lot of times, we think we have it all figured out, or we come to our own conclusions, but find out later that was not what He said, or what we thought He said, or what we figured out in our own minds that was what He meant. When He makes it clear to us, we think He has changed His mind. But it is not that at all. It is what He had established from the beginning before we were formed in our mother's womb. He had this plan, and an idea, and an identity and a purpose for us.

Walking it out in the now, for me, is walking in obedience, receiving a new key in the Kingdom. It is receiving a new key into my destiny that I didn't know I was going to need at this time, and I still don't know what I will need it for in the future. But He does, and I trust Him more than I ever have. I believe Him more, I understand Him better, and I walk in a much greater ability, a much better place, and have a much quicker response time than I ever have.

At this point, I have been married for 35 amazing years; I have four children, four children-in-law, seven grandchildren, and one on the way very, very soon. My life could not be much better than it is. But I know it is going to be because He never leaves us the same. I am definitely not the same as I was when He began with me, and I won't be the same when He is finished with me. I am still in the process of growing. It is still a progression; it is still from faith to faith, from everlasting to everlasting, and from glory to glory.

I can say that there have been seasons when I have been able to do and maintain the same things for almost 30 years straight, and it has been amazing. It has been an amazing journey. Now, I am in a season where God is saying, "Okay, we are going to readjust a few things. We are going to remodel. We might repurpose one or two things here. We are going to Kingdomize what needs to be Kingdomized." There is still some transforming and renewing of my mind going on regarding how I perceive things and how I do things; and really, the desires of my heart have changed as I have grown and matured.

I have learned much during all the lessons God taught me. I realize now that what I counted as a struggle, punishment, detour, mistake, or whatever I labeled them were actually opportunities God gave me to grow in places where I would not have grown if He had not given me those times of challenge. Not knowing that I needed to grow, not knowing that I needed strength in that place for the future, I would have missed what He had to teach me. God is so full of wisdom and compassion that He presented those circumstances knowing I needed to learn those lessons to prepare me for the future. Before I was aware that I needed His help, He was helping me.

When you really realize there has not been one thing about your life that He hasn't had His hand in or been part of or wasn't aware of, it's beyond our comprehension. He really and truly has used your life for His glory and for His Kingdom. Whether I have an understanding of it or not is on us.

> **His hand has been on every part of your life. He truly has used it for His glory and for His Kingdom.**

BYE BYE CRYBABY

Over the years I have grown in my understanding and have been able to change the lens of how I see, do, and process life. Instead of processing as a hurt, an offense, a rejection, or a disappointment, I see situations differently. All emotions were very much real to me because I am very much a feeler. I called myself a crybaby because it was very easy for people to hurt my feelings.

I always wanted to make everybody happy and do all of what goes with that personality type. Although not always healthy, I have learned that God used each one to bring me to the place where I am now. But I had to choose to partner with Him. I had to make a conscious decision to lay down my offenses, my hurts, my pain, my regrets, my shame, all that I carried so I could begin transforming and renewing my mind.

TRANSFORMATION AND RENEWAL

I had one of the greatest compliments given to me by one of the pastors I have known for almost 30 years as well. After going on a mission trip with me, he said that for many, many years he had seen people do mission trips the same way. Most say they don't want to Americanize people, so they go in and minimally help and take care of some of the people's needs. They don't want to change their culture or make things different.

I had heard that viewpoint too as we have traveled throughout the world, and it was hard for me to accept it. People don't understand why we do missions the way we do. We go in and build a completely different type of home. We go and build a high standard of schools. Our philosophy is that if what we build is not where we would want our kids to go to school or a house we would want them to live in, then it is not where these kids God has entrusted to us are going to live or attend school either. Our standard is to love people and transform places that we would want for our own children.

This pastor told me he had the privilege of taking care of and fixing and making improvements while on mission trips. But he said when he left, he really didn't think he made much of a difference.

Then he said, "The very first day on the trip with you guys, I didn't see people being Americanized—they were being Kingdomized!"

Kingdomized is such good language, because when you have an encounter with Jesus, He doesn't leave you the same. You don't look the same, you don't act the same. You now have a vision and a hope for the future that you never had. That is exactly what we get to do on the mission trips abroad as well as locally in people's lives we come in contact with. If people don't look different after you have an encounter with them, you have just wasted your time. You have not brought the Kingdom to them. We are transformed by the renewing of our minds through an encounter with Jesus—and He doesn't leave us the same way He found us.

Whenever Jesus healed people, they were no longer in need of healing. They were healed. They could walk, they could run, they could dance, they could see, and do all sorts of amazing feats. They no longer had bleeding issues or speaking problems. When Jesus forgave their sins, they were no longer sinners. When you see someone after they have accepted salvation, all of a sudden the person looks different. An inner joy shines through that shows on their face. That is what transformation is. That is what Kingdom is. That's what we are supposed to do as representatives of Jesus Himself.

And that is the place God brought me to. I can articulate that and say that and live that out loud. I can say that I am in a place I would have never imagined. I am in a place where I have my doctorate degree. I have a very successful ministry that I have worked in for many, many years. I see it grow and transform. I speak at events and conferences, and I do other ministry activities that I would never thought I would do. Honestly, I never wanted to do them.

These are not things I grew up thinking that I wanted to do. I was a "Background Barbara"—I wanted to be the one making things beautiful, the one nobody knew about, saw, or heard. I had the privilege and the ability to make things happen and take care of and love the "least of these" kids. I really thought that was what God called me to do.

But I have found that I have an even more abundant *life* in doing what He has called me to do. I have enjoyed traveling to more than 59 nations around the world to assist in transformation, speaking into government officials, and speaking to kings and queens. I am friends with people who need a friend and a mom and I am a mentor to those who need a mom and a mentor. That's the grace God has put on my life over the years and at this moment.

To be able to see people, really, truly see them the way Jesus sees them, has been the greatest gift God has given me. I now have a so much better understanding of when He was on the Cross, and He said, *"Father, forgive them for they know not what they do."* There are people who really, truly have no idea what they're doing when they are speaking against you or when they're bringing accusations or when they are hurt or offended. We've all made those mistakes, and we didn't know what we were doing.

But God loves us so much. He helps us mature. Then you get to the place in your walk or in your life where you can look at people who are still acting out in their pain and decide that you are not going to let their actions hurt your feelings anymore. You can decide to be like Jesus and say, "Father, please forgive them." You can remember, "I was that person, I walked there, I walked through that valley and the shadow of death. But You didn't leave me, Jesus. Please don't leave those people there." That is a remarkable place to be. I still have so far to go, but I know because of my experience with Him and because of my testimony of who God is, I'm going to get there.

NEVER, EVER

I have so many incredible testimonies of who God is to me, and one of them is that He has never, ever left me or forsaken me. He is my Healer. As a child, I had epilepsy, I had terrible seizures, I had terrible tragedies, I had many heartbreaks. But God never left me or forsook me. He healed me. He set me free. He set me apart. I grew up in situations and in areas that people without the Lord would not have made it through alive. Yet because of God, I blossomed in those circumstances. It was the blessed land of Goshen for my family (Genesis 12:7). God does what He does on purpose. He has a plan, and you can trust it if you truly have an eye to see it.

I'm grateful that God has been so patient and kind with me. He has given me eyes to see. The older I get I'm like Moses, my eyes are not growing dim, even though I have to wear readers to read, but my spiritual eyes have not grown dim. I can see better, I can understand better, and I trust more. I can love deeper than I've ever been able to in my entire existence, and I'm so grateful for that.

The last thing I'm going to leave with you is that anytime God gives you an opportunity to sow mercy, do. What I mean by that is there is someone who needs your mercy, even if you don't think the person deserves it. Maybe you need to show mercy because they've done something to you, or maybe they don't appreciate what you did for them, or maybe God has put someone in your life you really don't like. But God wants you to have mercy on them. Maybe you are thinking they don't need mercy. They are mean, miserable, ungrateful, or whatever. But God really wants you to show them mercy.

When you extend mercy because of the goodness of God and out of your obedience to Him, you can know you are banking mercy. You will have mercy in your spiritual bank account. Then one day, when you need someone to show you mercy, you can to tap into your account. You have mercy stored up right there, and you can cash it in.

Maybe it's forgiveness God is telling you to give someone. We all need forgiveness from time to time. No one is right all the time and no one other than Jesus was perfect. So, we need people to forgive us. And we need to forgive others. It is truly a sin not to forgive, so we have to forgive, and be willing to forgive. When we forgive people we don't think deserve it, we are banking forgiveness. You will have deposited forgiveness into your spiritual bank account.

That principle is true for every part of your life: grace, faithfulness, or whatever. Sow into all the blessings you will need in your life. Bank in every part of your life. He knows your tomorrows and what you're going to need from your spiritual bank account. He is continually giving you opportunities to make deposits so that ten years down the road, when you really need Him to show up, you will have what you need. Or maybe you are going to need it to give to someone else. Whatever it is, you can always trust Him with everything you are. You can trust Him with your family, your children, your life, your marriage, your ministry, and you can trust His promises. His ways are so much greater than our ways. His heart of love for us is so much more incredible than we can hope or imagine.

I pray that this book finds you blessed and that it has encouraged you and helped you see your life through a very different lens than you have seen before. I hope it has shown you new things about the beauty of who you are, that it has shown you how beautiful you are to Him, and how spectacular and blessed you truly are.

To be continued...

SECTION NINE

Shepherd My Soul

*Personal Reflections
from the Book*

Introduction

When we read the stories of people and events in the Bible, we hear God's voice speaking to us. He is always speaking to us—certainly through the Bible, but also through what is happening around us in the people and events in our lives. It is important for us to take time to listen.

The "Shepherd Your Soul" section provides an opportunity to reflect on Pastor Leanna's life and seek the Good Shepherd to hear what He is saying to *you* through her story. In this section there are Scriptures and questions to guide your conversations with Him. All are offered as possible suggestions—the Holy Spirit may prompt others for you.

HOW TO USE THIS SECTION

From the Text: Each reflection time is based on a quotation from the book.

Consider: This is a short teaching to clarify or focus the spiritual work.

Scriptures: These verses address the topic and may prompt you to search out others as well. Spend time absorbing the verses, allowing each to do their work in you.

Remember: *"See, the Word of God is alive! It is at work and is sharper than any double-edged sword—it cuts right through to where soul meets spirit and joints meet marrow, and it is quick to judge the inner reflections and attitudes of the heart"* (Hebrews 4:12 CJB).

God-Talk: There are some *examples of questions* for you to ask the Lord. There may be others in your soul that the Holy Spirit will show you.

Heart-Work: Your heart is where your soul joins with your spirit. Your soul is where your thoughts, feelings, and your will reside. Before you were born again, your spirit was the spirit of man; now it is the Holy Spirit. Many old thoughts, feelings, and most of our will are based on our worldly experiences. They are being transformed by the Holy Spirit out of worldly influence into Kingdom influence. This section has focus questions to work on what is stored in your heart.

All of this work is to be Holy-Spirit led, and each section saves the most important part for last. Allow time to ask this question and abundant time to sit with the One who loves you best and truly listen to Him.

So, *from your open, willing, and listening heart...***ask:**

Holy Spirit, what are You saying to me through this lesson?

From the Field to the Palace

FROM THE TEXT

To me, the title, *She Shepherd*, is my life. It is part of what makes me who I am. It is who I am, loving what I do, and being authentically me. I think all of us should be who we are. God only made one of each of us.

He only made one of you, so you should be yourself; everyone else is taken. I want to encourage you to seek out who you are and be okay with that.

The greatest part of that story is Ruth's faithfulness. Her undying love, her undying dedication, her steadfastness, her ability to lay down her life. She laid it all aside because she truly loved. She truly believed that God was good and that He was calling her to be her mother-in-law's daughter. She did that; she laid it all down when it wasn't easy or fun, when her mother-in-law was sad, when the culture was different. When all was against her, she did everything her mother-in-law told her.

CONSIDER

What is your unique story and true identity? Maybe you are in a unique role that others never consider. Maybe you are in a normal role but walking it out uniquely. Our Father created 17,500 species of butterflies just for the sheer delight of having them in the world. How much more does He fill His Kingdom with delightful children?

Like Ruth had for Naomi, we need a heart yielded to God's will to carry out His plan. Ruth submitted in the fields of hard labor and through her son, Obed, she became part of the royal family of our King Jesus. Be authentically who He created you to be because *"No eye has seen, no ear has heard, and no mind has imagined what God has prepared for those who love him"* (1 Corinthians 2:9 NLT).

SCRIPTURES

...Orpah kissed her mother-in-law good-bye. But Ruth clung tightly to Naomi. "Look," Naomi said to her, "your sister-in-law has gone back to her people and to her gods. You should do the same." But Ruth replied, "Don't ask me to leave you and turn back. Wherever you go, I will go; wherever you live, I will live. Your people will be my people, and your God will be my God. Wherever you die, I will die, and there I will be buried. May the Lord punish me severely if I allow anything but death to separate us!" When Naomi saw that Ruth was determined to go with her, she said nothing more (Ruth 1:14-18 NLT).

After Boaz married Ruth,

The neighbor women said, "Now at last Naomi has a son again!" And they named him Obed. He became the father of Jesse and the grandfather of David (Ruth 4:17 NLT).

GOD-TALK

- Father, what do You want me to know about the fullness of me that You created?
- Father, if You had a title for me, what would it be?
- Jesus, what do You want to say to me about what true love is?

HEART-WORK

Holy Spirit, come and fill me to overflow, mold me into the image of My Father, and set me on the path with Jesus.

From your open, willing, and listening heart, **ask:**

Holy Spirit, what are You saying to me through this lesson?

Demonstration That Overcomes

FROM THE TEXT

Now that I am an adult who has kids and grandkids, I'm amazed at what our parents did. It's a wonder to me that they had the ability to keep us so pure and so innocent in the midst of "Egypt." We lived in the midst of the roughest places, and yet, we had no clue about the world around us there.

Both of my parents were really good demonstrators. They weren't just preachers of the Gospel—they were demonstrators of the Gospel.

CONSIDER

Christians live in this world, but our minds are fixed on Jesus's Kingdom; we are in the world but not of the world. The way to impact our families, our friends, and the world is to demonstrate how to live by Kingdom principles and walk in the love of Christ.

SCRIPTURES

> *Do not be overcome by evil, but overcome evil with good* (Romans 12:21 NKJV).

> *Imitate God, therefore, in everything you do, because you are His dear children. Live a life filled with love, following the example of Christ. He loved us and offered himself as a sacrifice for us, a pleasing aroma to God* (Ephesians 5:1-2 NLT).

> *So be careful how you live. Don't live like fools, but like those who are wise. Make the most of every opportunity in these evil days. Don't act thoughtlessly, but understand what the Lord wants you to do* (Ephesians 5:15-17 NLT).

And give thanks for everything to God the Father in the name of our Lord Jesus Christ (Ephesians 5:20 NLT).

GOD-TALK

- God, am I demonstrating Your goodness so those around me will be touched by it? Will You show me how I can improve?
- Jesus, will You show me any evil around me that is drawing my attention away from Your Kingdom?
- Lord, what do You want to say to me about the environment of my home?

HEART-WORK

- Holy Spirit, is there anything ungodly stored in my soul that came in during my childhood?
- What do You want to show me or say to me about that?
- Lord, will You strengthen my will to do Your will in my life?

From your open, willing, and listening heart, **ask:**

Holy Spirit, what are You saying to me through this lesson?

Watch Where You Are Going

FROM THE TEXT

The safest place you can be is in the will of God. It doesn't matter where you live, it doesn't matter what you have, it doesn't matter who you know; the safest place is in the will of God. So, finding out His will and His heart is the greatest gift you can give your kids. It was the greatest gift given to me. It is important to focus on knowing the will of God. Don't focus on things that aren't of Him. If you are saying, "That's the devil's music, that's the devil's this, or that's the devil's that," you have the wrong focus. What you look at is where you are going.

CONSIDER

When you look for God's will for yourself or your children, you won't find it in the devil. When all we are looking at is the devil and his work in the world around us, we miss what God is saying to us. Our God is the creative Creator, and when we connect our thoughts to His and consider His Kingdom agenda, He can show us great and mysterious things we don't know. Look upon those things.

SCRIPTURES

Finally, brethren, whatever things are true, whatever things are noble, whatever things are just, whatever things are pure, whatever things are lovely, whatever things are of good report, if there is any virtue and if there is anything praiseworthy—meditate on these things (Philippians 4:8 NKJV).

...And let us run with endurance the race God has set before us. We do this by keeping our eyes on Jesus, the champion who initiates and perfects our faith. Because of the joy awaiting him, He endured the cross, disregarding its shame. Now, He is seated in the place of honor beside God's throne (Hebrews 12:1-2 NLT).

GOD-TALK

- Jesus, where do You want me to focus my thoughts? Where am I off base?

- Father, where do You want to lead me? Will You clearly mark the path You want me to take?

- Holy Spirit, what is in my heart that needs to be removed so I can keep my eyes on Jesus?

HEART-WORK:

- God, what do You want me to know about things I have stored in my soul that came in through evil influences?
- Holy Spirit, send Your cleansing fire to remove anything not of Jesus from my memory and my feelings and strengthen my will to focus on Him and Him alone.

From your open, willing, and listening heart, **ask:**

Holy Spirit, what are You saying to me through this lesson?

Love Is a Choice

FROM THE TEXT

When I met Troy, he had a little girl. When we decided to get married, it meant that I was going to be a stepmom. My thought was, *I do not want to be a wicked stepmother.* I remember talking to my mom about this. I came to her and said, "Mom, I'm really concerned that I am not going to be as good of a mom to her as I should be because I am going to be a stepmom." My mom told me, "You choose who you love."

She reminded me of all the kids I grew up with and all the kids they had parented and continue to parent. You can't tell who was biological and who wasn't. We all grew up the same; they loved us all the same. I absolutely love our daughter. I loved her before she was my daughter.

CONSIDER

The text is from a section on blended families. You may not have a blended family, but there may be similar situations in your work, church, or neighborhood where we are "blended together" with others and where these teachings apply.

Blended families often offer many challenges, but they are still God's family. As part of the family of God, we are commanded to love all people. If you have any children in your life, biologically yours or not, you are charged with loving and nurturing them in a way that is pleasing to the Lord. We are also called to be peacemakers as much as we possibly can and that means in relationships with the child's other set of parents.

Jesus chose to love us. The apostle Paul wrote in Romans 5:8 (NKJV), *"God demonstrates His own love toward us, in that while we were still sinners, Christ died for us."* We may not always agree with the other parents, but we are called to be peacemakers and to act in love in all our dealings with them because we have chosen to love the same child.

SCRIPTURES

A new commandment I give to you, that you love one another; as I have loved you, that you also love one another.

By this all will know that you are My disciples, if you have love for one another (John 13:34-35 NKJV).

But if you love those who love you, what credit is that to you? For even sinners love those who love them (Luke 6:32 NKJV).

GOD-TALK

- God, please show me where personalities or situations with people are keeping me from fulfilling the commandment You gave me to love others.

- Jesus, teach me to love others the way You do.

HEART-WORK

- Holy Spirit, lead me into all Truth about what is in my heart about blended relationships in my life.

- Cleanse my heart of impure attitudes and resentments.

- Convict me of any sin and turn my heart to the ways of Jesus as I repent.

From your open, willing, and listening heart, **ask:**

Holy Spirit, what are You saying to me through this lesson?

New Walk

FROM THE TEXT

She said, "I don't want to wear these anymore. I don't want to wear these anymore." And I said, "You don't have to wear them anymore."

Then she looked at me and said, "Will you please be my mama?" Oh my, that made me cry. And I said, "Yes, of course I will. I will be your mama." I asked her if I could pray for her. I prayed for her and led her to the Lord.

The Lord told me, "I want you to take your shoes off your feet and give them to her because she's going to have a different walk." Your shoes represent your walk. I said, "Yes, Lord, I will." Then I looked down and saw my Jerusalem shoes. I thought, *Wow, Lord, You knew what I was going to be doing with these. I didn't know, but of course You did.* And I gave her my shoes. It wasn't just that I gave her my shoes—they were special shoes that meant something to me. The Lord was telling me that her walk was changing forever.

CONSIDER

When we encounter Jesus, we are made completely new. Our circumstances and the people around us may be the same, but He has given us a new walk. It is important to see yourself wearing new shoes and going in a different direction, on a new path that will keep you in close contact with Jesus. The Holy Spirit comes inside you to help remind you of the truth and guide you down the new path. The Bible is your new GPS—it is God's positioning system to keep you walking with Jesus, so study it.

SCRIPTURES

This means that anyone who belongs to Christ has become a new person. The old life is gone; a new life has begun! (2 Corinthians 5:17 NLT)

Therefore we were buried with Him through baptism into death, that just as Christ was raised from the dead by the glory of the Father, even so we also should walk in newness of life (Romans 6:4 NKJV).

GOD-TALK

- Jesus, what do You want to say to me about my walk?
- Holy Spirit, will You show me areas where I need to change direction?

HEART-WORK

- Holy Spirit, is there anything in my heart that is keeping me from a close relationship with Jesus?

- Jesus, will You come and wash my spiritual feet and remove any dust from things from my past that is still in my heart?

From your open, willing, and listening heart, **ask:**

Holy Spirit, what are You saying to me through this lesson?

Blessed to Be a Blessing

FROM THE TEXT

He saves us and redeems us so we can live with Him and join Him in Kingdom work. He loves to give to us, and as we grow in our relationship with Him, He will use us to give to others. He blesses us so we can be a blessing to others.

CONSIDER

When we are saved and redeemed, we have been born again into a new life, and that new life is in God's Kingdom. Our physical self is still in the world, but our soul is no longer *of* the world. We have a new Kingdom identity that reflects our identity in Christ.

Just like in the physical world, we may look like our parents and begin to act the way they act. After spiritual birth, we begin to look more like God in everything we do as He continues to reveal to us who He truly is.

Because He loves us, He has given abundantly to us. He gave us life, He gave His Son to redeem us, and He lavishly provides all we need and want. Does your life reflect our Father as the giving God?

SCRIPTURES

I will make you a great nation; I will bless you and make your name great; and you shall be a blessing. I will bless those who bless you, and I will curse him who curses you; and in you all the families of the earth shall be blessed (Genesis 12:2-3 NKJV).

The person who blesses others will prosper; he who satisfies others will be satisfied himself (Proverbs 11:25 CJB).

You will be enriched in every way, so that you can be generous in everything (2 Corinthians 9:11 CJB).

He who is kind to the poor is lending to Adonai, and he will repay him for his good deed (Proverbs 19:17 CJB).

GOD-TALK

- Lord, how do You think I look like You?

- What areas of my life best show others who You are?

- God, what do You want to say to me about blessing others?

HEART-WORK

- Ask Holy Spirit to search your heart and show you any lies you believe about being generous.

- Jesus says He is the Light. Ask Him to show you any places where your ideas or thoughts about the poor or people who are different or less fortunate than you are don't align with Him.

From your open, willing, and listening heart, **ask:**

Holy Spirit, what are You saying to me through this lesson?

His Word Does Not Return Void

FROM THE TEXT

The Lord recalled incidents from my childhood that helped me understand His hand had always been on my life. I was hit by a car when I was 2 and by another one when I was 8; I drowned two different times, and I had epilepsy during my childhood. Recalling all of that helped convince my heart that He had set me apart "for such a time" as I was entering (Esther 4:14).

CONSIDER

When God formed us in our mother's womb, He had a purpose for our lives. He is not a random God. Even before we knew about God, He knew about us. He loved us before we loved Him.

When we consider that, we can know that whether we knew it or not, He was shepherding our lives. He created everything through a word; He spoke us into being by calling our name. In that moment, His plan for our life was set into motion and carried out.

When we called out His name for our salvation, it opened the door for us to walk in His plan. There is a reason we are here at this time. There is no other you. There is no other time, just like the one we are in.

Consider the fact that God created you specifically to answer a call, meet a need, touch a soul, or in some other marvelous way, to fit into His divine plan.

SCRIPTURES

For you fashioned my inmost being; you knit me together in my mother's womb. I thank you because I am awesomely made, wonderfully; your works are wonders—I know this very well.

My bones were not hidden from you when I was being made in secret, intricately woven in the depths of the earth. Your eyes could see me as an embryo, but in your book, all my days were already written; my days had been shaped before any of them existed. God, how I prize your thoughts! How many of them there are! (Psalm 139:13-17 CJB)

No weapon formed against you shall prosper (Isaiah 54:17 NKJV).

For just as rain and snow fall from the sky and do not return there, but water the earth, causing it to bud and produce, giving seed to the sower and bread to the eater; so is my word that goes out from my mouth—it will not return to me unfulfilled; but it will accomplish what I intend, and cause to succeed what I sent it to do (Isaiah 55:10-11 CJB).

For if you remain completely silent at this time, relief and deliverance will arise for the Jews from another place, but you and your father's house will perish. Yet who knows whether you have come to the kingdom for such a time as this? (Esther 4:14 NKJV).

GOD-TALK

- God, am I set apart by You?

- Lord, will You show me times from my childhood when You were present and I didn't realize You were there? What do You want to tell me about those experiences?

- Holy Spirit, where do I fit into Your plan? What do You want me to know about Your purpose for me?

- Lord Jesus, how can I participate with You to bring what You have spoken into being?

HEART-WORK

- Holy Spirit, please show me anything in me that needs to die and be removed so God's will can be done in my life.

- Ask to see any playgrounds, playmates, or playlists that are keeping you bound to the world instead of walking in your purpose.

- God, who will benefit from what You have called me to do?

- Lord Jesus, will You give me courage and strengthen my voice?

From your open, willing, and listening heart, **ask:**

Holy Spirit, what are You saying to me through this lesson?

He Equips the Called

FROM THE TEXT

The Lord knew I felt unsure about my ability to have a ministry, and He used the encounter with the bushman that day to show me that I only needed Him to reach others.

CONSIDER

At the beginning of 2024, as a church, OpenDoor focused our attention on Psalm 24. It begins with, *"The earth is the Lord's, and all its fullness, the world and those who dwell therein."* (NKJV). When we have the mindset that everything and everyone belongs to the Lord, it impacts our understanding of having a call on our lives.

We have a purpose to work within *His* ministry. None of us have a "ministry." We all have an assignment in His ministry. He is a wonderful Leader, and no matter what, He will understand. He is patient with us as we develop. He wants us to be successful—even more than we want that. He will not set us up to fail.

SCRIPTURES

Being confident of this very thing, that He which hath begun a good work in you will perform it until the day of Jesus Christ (Philippians 1:6 NKJV).

And God is able to make all grace abound toward you, that you, always having all sufficiency in all things, may have an abundance for every good work (2 Corinthians 9:8 NKJV).

May that God equip you with every good thing you need to do his will; and may he do in us whatever pleases him, through Yeshua the Messiah. To him be the glory forever and ever. Amen (Hebrews 13:21 CJB).

GOD-TALK

- Holy Spirit, will You please remind me of some of the lessons You have taught me in the past?

- What do You want me to see about those lessons?

- God, what do You wish I knew that I don't know?

- Jesus, will You show me some of the ways You want me to minister with You in the future?

HEART-WORK

- Holy Spirit, will You speak to me about my confidence level in what You want me to do?

- What do You want to tell me about why I lack confidence?

- Jesus, will You minister to my heart so it is strong and full of confidence?

From your open, willing, and listening heart, **ask:**

Holy Spirit, what are You saying to me through this lesson?

I Am Hungry

FROM THE TEXT

There were thousands of people in attendance, and Troy was about to go onto the stage to preach. He was in an area that was roped off from the people attending. It was terribly noisy, and security personnel were standing by the roped-off area. Nevertheless, a little boy managed to get through the crowd of people and the security, and he went up right up to Troy and said, "Sir, you must feed me, for I am hungry," he said respectfully but loud enough to be heard over all the noise.

CONSIDER

Can you imagine being so desperate for what you needed that you defied all obstacles standing between you and the person you knew would be your salvation? This young boy went after what he had to have with a no-matter-what approach. Nothing would keep him from Pastor Troy. Most of us have never been hungry; we've never known the gnawing ache inside for what we had to have to sustain our lives.

Our bellies may have never known that ache, but at one time our souls have. Our souls are desperately hungry for Jesus. We have to have Jesus to live. Ecclesiastes 3:11 says God has put eternity into human hearts. Are you desperate for Him in a no-matter-what-it-takes way? Are you willing to cry out for Him and tell Him what you need from Him no matter who tries to stop you?

SCRIPTURES

Then it happened, as He was coming near Jericho, that a certain blind man sat by the road begging. And hearing a multitude passing by, he asked what it meant. So they told him that Jesus of Nazareth was passing by. And he cried out, saying, "Jesus, Son of David, have mercy on me!"

Then those who went before warned him that he should be quiet; but he cried out all the more, "Son of David, have mercy on me!" So Jesus stood still and commanded him to be brought to Him. And when he had come near, He asked him, saying, "What do you want Me to do for you?" He said, "Lord, that I may receive my sight." Then Jesus said to him, "Receive your sight; your faith has made you well." And immediately he received His sight, and followed Him, glorifying God. And all the people, when they saw it, gave praise to God (Luke 18:35-43 NKJV).

GOD-TALK

- God, will You come nearer to me and let me feel Your presence in a new way?

- Jesus, I am desperate for You because… (you complete this sentence).

- Holy Spirit, am I letting what other people think have an influence on my relationship with Jesus?

HEART-WORK

- Holy Spirit, will You speak to me about my beliefs?
- Will You show me any place where I lack trust in Jesus to do things I ask of Him?

From your open, willing, and listening heart, **ask:**

Holy Spirit, what are You saying to me through this lesson?

True Religion

FROM THE TEXT

We took Colin with us to meet several pastors from this big crusade to eat together. They saw us walking up with this little boy and began to try to shoo him away. We said, "No, he's with us. He isn't a random child following us. He is with us." They said, "You can't bring him with you."

We said, "Yes, we can. He is with us. He is hungry, and we are going to feed him." They said, "But you don't know him." We explained that he was an orphan and that we had gone to where he lived. Feeling like they just didn't understand, we said, "He is all by himself, and there is nobody. It isn't like we are going to get into trouble for taking this little boy. He doesn't have parents, grandparents, or anybody. He is living on the streets."

One pastor turned to us and said, "There are thousands of them." Troy quickly replied, "I don't know thousands of them. But I know this one. This one is no longer going to be an orphan; he is ours, and he is going to dinner with us." The pastors didn't appreciate this.

CONSIDER

Two pastors in this text saw a young orphan boy in need and responded with a Yes! There was a cause to act in the way Jesus modeled. They answered the need with action to meet not only the immediate need but also to step into the future of this boy and change his narrative.

Several pastors saw the need, turned away from the boy and did nothing; worse yet, they tried to dissuade Pastors Troy and Leanna from acting on the boy's behalf.

Which type of religious observance do you follow?

SCRIPTURES

Don't deceive yourselves by only hearing what the Word says, but do it! ...The religious observance that God the Father considers pure and faultless is this: to care for orphans and widows in their distress and to keep oneself from being contaminated by the world (James 1:22, 27 CJB).

Then the people who have done what God wants will reply, "Lord, when did we see you hungry and feed you, or thirsty and give you something to drink? When did we see you a stranger and make you our guest, or needing clothes and provide them? When did we see you sick or in prison, and visit you?" The King will say to them, "Yes! I tell you that whenever you did these things for one of the least important of these brothers of mine, you did them for me!" Then he will also speak to those on his left, saying, "Get away from me, you who are cursed! Go off into the fire prepared for the Adversary and his angels! For I was hungry and you gave me no food, thirsty and you gave me nothing to drink, a stranger and you did not welcome me, needing clothes and you did not give them to me, sick and in prison and you did not visit me." Then they too will reply, "Lord, when did we see you hungry, thirsty, a stranger, needing clothes, sick or in prison, and not take care of you?" And he will answer them, "Yes! I tell you that whenever you refused to do it for the least important of these people, you refused to do it for me!" They will go off to eternal punishment, but those who have done what God wants will go to eternal life (Matthew 25:37-46 CJB).

GOD-TALK

- Jesus, what do You want to say to me about how I have responded to needs I see?
- Is there anything about my past actions I need to confess and repent so I can receive forgiveness?

- Holy Spirit, will You show me an area where I can reach out and help others?

HEART-WORK

- Holy Spirit, will You remove any religious spirit from my soul?
- Will You show me where that came in and impacted my beliefs?
- Jesus, will You fill my heart with Your love for the people of the world?

From your open, willing, and listening heart, **ask:**

Holy Spirit, what are You saying to me through this lesson?

I Came Praying

FROM THE TEXT

The whole time all this was going on, Jimmy just smiled. He just loves Jesus; he loves, loves Jesus. Dr. Noah said, "Jimmy, do you know that God sent these people from the West to take care of you?"

Jimmy smiled and said, "Yes, I know. I came praying."

In that moment, I thought, *If I had that kind of faith, if I had the kind of faith that Jimmy had, what could I do? What difference could I make? Jimmy **believed**.*"

CONSIDER

This young orphan boy lived on the ground and scavenged for food. Some people might say he had nothing. Those of us who know the Lord intimately, know this boy had found the unfading, inexhaustible riches of Christ.

SCRIPTURES

> *I have been made a messenger of this wonderful news by the gift of grace that works through me. Even though I am the least significant of all his holy believers, this grace-gift was imparted when the manifestation of his power came upon me. Grace alone empowers me so that I can boldly preach this wonderful message to non-Jewish people, sharing with them the unfading, inexhaustible riches of Christ, which are beyond comprehension* (Ephesians 3:7-8 TPT).

> *So Jesus answered and said to them, "Have faith in God. For assuredly, I say to you, whoever says to this mountain, 'Be removed and be cast into the sea,' and does not doubt in his heart but believes that those things he says will be done, he will have whatever he says. Therefore, I say to you whatever things you ask when you pray, believe that you receive them, and you will have them"* (Mark 11:22-24 NKJV).

GOD-TALK

- God, I want to know You better. Please tell me about the unfading, inexhaustible riches of Christ.
- Lord, what do You want me to know about my level of faith?
- Jesus, will You release a grace-gift to me through Your power You placed in me through Your Holy Spirit?
- If you are ready to believe, speak to your mountain.

HEART-WORK

- Holy Spirit, please reveal any doubt or unbelief I have in my heart and show me the root.
- As I understand the root, please tell me Your truth so I no longer believe the lies.

From your open, willing, and listening heart, **ask:**

Holy Spirit, what are You saying to me through this lesson?

Miracles, Signs, and Wonders

FROM THE TEXT

We prayed for this lady who had been completely bent over for most of her life. There are no schools out there, and the children go to work in the gardens from the time they are very young. She was stuck in that bent-over position and couldn't stand up. I prayed for her, and the power of prayer there was incredible.

Then I went back to meet with this man who owns the land. He hadn't been to any of our "tree meetings." He was a Muslim man, and he walked out, and a woman walked with him. I didn't recognize the woman who was walking with him.

He said, "I don't believe in your God, but my wife has been bent over for many, many years, and you prayed for her, and she is healed." The reason I didn't recognize the woman with him was that now she was standing up straight.

CONSIDER

Some denominations in the body of the church today teach that spiritual gifts ceased with the Age of Apostles. When Jesus walked the earth, He healed all who came to Him and did miracles, signs, and wonders to show His divinity. Many came to believe because of them.

Just before being crucified, Jesus prayed for His disciples and *all who will ever believe* because of their work; that means all of us. The

Gospel came forth because of the apostles' work; so if we believe, it is because they kept His message alive, and miraculous signs followed them. He intends that to continue until He returns.

SCRIPTURES

I am praying not only for these disciples but also for all who will ever believe in me through their message. I pray that they will all be one, just as you and I are one—as you are in me, Father, and I am in you. And may they be in us so that the world will believe you sent me (John 17:20-21 NLT).

And then he told them, "Go into all the world and preach the Good News to everyone. Anyone who believes and is baptized will be saved. But anyone who refuses to believe will be condemned. These miraculous signs will accompany those who believe: They will cast out demons in my name, and they will speak in new languages. They will be able to handle snakes with safety, and if they drink anything poisonous, it won't hurt them. They will be able to place their hands on the sick, and they will be healed." When the Lord Jesus had finished talking with them, he was taken up into heaven and sat down in the place of honor at God's right hand. And the disciples went everywhere and preached, and the Lord worked through them, confirming what they said by many miraculous signs (Mark 16:15-20 NLT).

GOD-TALK

- Jesus, I believe, help my unbelief. Will you show me any attitudes I may have that keep me from operating in miracles, signs, and wonders?

- If you need healing for anything in your life, talk to Jesus about that. Ask Him your specific questions and listen carefully to His responses.

- If you don't need healing, talk to Jesus about people on your prayer list who do.

- God, please allow me to walk fully in all the spiritual gifts You have for me.

- God, what do You want to say to me about the gifts?

HEART-WORK

- Holy Spirit, will You reveal any thoughts and beliefs I have that came from false teaching?

- Jesus, will You heal any broken places in my heart that came because the healing I wanted didn't come?

- What do You want to show me about those situations?

From your open, willing, and listening heart, **ask:**

Holy Spirit, what are You saying to me through this lesson?

Fitting Through the Door

FROM THE TEXT

Many times, to be able to fit through the door that God has opened for you, you have to get still, and you have to get small. There's a Scripture about the camel fitting through the eye of the needle (Matthew 19:24), which is an opening in a city's wall that is a little door. The camel has to kneel down and crawl through it to be able to go through the wall and enter into the city.

Sometimes we have to get humble to be able to fit through these open doors. We may have to acknowledge that it may not be the way we think it should be; it may not look the way we think it should look. Being able to humble yourself and say, "Okay, God, I really do believe that You love me with all Your heart. I believe Your intentions for me are good. I believe Your heart toward me is good." The Scripture says that He has plans for us and that they are for our good (Jeremiah 29:11). Sometimes, we forget that, therefore, we think we have to protect ourselves. Protecting ourselves from Jesus is never the right answer. It's a lie; it's a trick and a deception.

CONSIDER

The eye of the needle was a narrow opening in the wall around Jerusalem. For a camel to fit through, all the goods and the riders were removed, and the camels could crawl through the opening. We too may have to unload many things to fit through the doors God opens.

SCRIPTURES

Jesus said to His disciples, "I assure you and most solemnly say to you, it is difficult for a rich man [who clings to possessions and status as security] to enter the kingdom of heaven. Again I tell you, it is easier for a camel to go through the eye of a needle, than for a rich man [who places his faith in wealth and status] to enter the kingdom of God" (Matthew 19:23-24 Amplified Bible).

GOD-TALK

- God, will You show me what burdens, possessions, and attachments to other people or other things I need to unload to walk through the doors You have opened?
- Jesus, will You give me a vision or show me Your plan for me?
- Holy Spirit, will You reveal expectations I have that don't align with Your plan for my life?

HEART-WORK

- Holy Spirit, tell me the ways I am trying to protect myself and show me the root of that.
- Lord, set me free from anything keeping me in bondage outside Your will.

From your open, willing, and listening heart, **ask:**

Holy Spirit, what are You saying to me through this lesson?

Pick a Side—Yours, Mine, or His

FROM THE TEXT

I was a young woman in ministry, and we were going through a very hard time in ministry. I remember going to him and saying, "Dad, this is what happened. It's not fair, I don't know what to do." I was pouring my heart out and he stopped me. He said, "There are three sides to every story." When he said that, I thought, *Oh, great, he's gonna say something crazy like he always does.*

He said, "There's your side, there's their side, and then there's the truth." I told him that wasn't helping me right now. I said, "I need you to hear me; I need you to be on my side on this; I need you to tell me I'm right." I knew I was right, but it wasn't about being right. Of course, my dad was actually right. He said you need to stick to truth.

Jesus is the truth, He's the way, He's the truth, and He's life. If you don't stick with the truth, it doesn't matter if you're right or wrong.

CONSIDER

There will be times of discord with other people. It is not some-thing we want, but because we are all still human, it will happen occasionally. We have to decide whether we will pick up an offense and defend our position—or will we seek Jesus. We can ask Him to speak into the matter. We can ask Him to direct our steps so we do the next right thing in every situation.

SCRIPTURES

Bless those who persecute you. Don't curse them; pray that God will bless them. Be happy with those who are happy, and weep with those who weep. Live in harmony with each other. Don't be too proud to enjoy the company of ordinary people. And don't think you know it all! Never pay back evil with more evil. Do things in such a way that everyone can see you are honorable. Do all that you can to live in peace with everyone (Romans 12:14-18 NLT).

GOD-TALK

- If you have unforgiveness or offense in your heart, spend time with Jesus today and ask Him to speak to you about it. Tell Him all that is in your heart about the situation, and listen to what He says.

- Lord, will You show me things I don't know and understand about unresolved issues?

- Seek the Lord for any pressing issue in your life today; seek His way, His truth, and ask Him to breathe life into the issue.

HEART-WORK

- Ask for more of the Holy Spirit to be poured out in you, and open up to experience all the blessings of the Spirit.

From your open, willing, and listening heart, **ask:**

Holy Spirit, what are You saying to me through this lesson?

Jewish Jesus

FROM THE TEXT

Understanding the Jewish culture has been really good for me, and it's been a blessing to delve into the customs and the culture of Jewish Jesus, and I love Him even more. I love everything about Him. I love the culture over there. I love their understanding of family. There is a different understanding of the family in the Jewish culture than anything I've ever seen.

CONSIDER

When Jesus returns, He comes as the joyful Bridegroom, and the church will meet Him as His bride. That means we are all grafted in as part of the Jewish family. The Jewish families value their time together and make family the priority. The Bible stories teach us how important family is to God. Living in a Western culture has taken a great deal away from our sense of family life.

If we make restoring God-honoring families a priority, we have Scriptures, the Holy Spirit, and wisdom from above to show us how.

SCRIPTURES

For this reason, I fall on my knees before the Father, from whom every family in heaven and on earth receives its character. I pray that from the treasures of His glory He will empower you with inner strength by his Spirit, so that the Messiah may live in your hearts through your trusting. Also I pray that you will be rooted and founded in love, so that you, with all God's people, will be given strength to grasp the breadth, length, height, and depth of the Messiah's love, yes, to know it, even though it is beyond all knowing, so that you will be filled with all the fullness of God. Now to him who by His power working in us is able to do far beyond anything we can ask or imagine, to him be glory in the Messianic Community and in the Messiah Yeshua from generation to generation forever. Amen (Ephesians 3:14-21 CJB).

GOD-TALK

- Father, show me how to honor You through my family life.
- What do You want me to know about changing my heart and mind about my family and all families?
- Jesus, will You open my heart to love Israel like You do?

HEART-WORK

- Holy Spirit, search my heart and show me any place I believe a lie about the Jewish faith.

- Please show me the root of that and remove it completely from my life.
- Jesus, come and set me free from any old ways of living as a family, and show me Your ways.

From your open, willing, and listening heart, **ask:**

Holy Spirit, what are You saying to me through this lesson?

We Will Remember

FROM THE TEXT

If you go to Israel, don't miss touring Yad Vashem, The World Holocaust Remembrance Center in Jerusalem. It was emotionally hard for me seeing the faces and reading about the millions of Jews who were murdered during World War II. As I walked through the hallways, a voice was saying, "We will not forget. We will not forget." That is one of the commandments of the Lord.

Jewish people know the Torah, know who they are, and know where they come from. It goes back to identity. They know who they are because they know who God is and they remember Him.

CONSIDER

We are made in God's image. The more we know Him as our Father, the more we understand our identity. The more we remember who He is and what He has done in the past, the more we will begin to shape our identity to His.

SCRIPTURES

Remember Who God Is

> For I will proclaim the name of Adonai. Come, declare the greatness of our God! The Rock! His work is perfect, for all His ways are just. A trustworthy God who does no wrong, He is righteous and straight (Deuteronomy 32:3-4 CJB).

Remember What God Has Done

> Remember things that happened at the beginning, long ago—that I am God, and there is no other; I am God, and there is none like me. At the beginning, I announce the end, proclaim in advance things not yet done; and I say that my plan will hold, I will do everything I please to do (Isaiah 46:9-10 CJB).

Remember His Promises

> Therefore, go and make people from all nations into talmidim, immersing them into the reality of the Father, the Son and the Ruach HaKodesh, and teaching them to obey everything that I have commanded you. And remember! I

will be with you always, yes, even until the end of the age
(Matthew 28:19-20 CJB).

GOD-TALK

- Jesus, show our Father to me in a new way. Remind me who He has always been to me.
- Father, don't let me forget the ways You have shown me You love me. Call them to my mind today.
- Holy Spirit, remind me of all of the promises of Jesus.

HEART-WORK

- Holy Spirit, reveal any fear, doubt, or worry that is in my soul because I have forgotten God's faithfulness. Help me repent and replace those with love, trust, and faith in God.
- Jesus, what do You want me to know about anything in my past that is stored in my heart?

From your open, willing, and listening heart, **ask:**

Holy Spirit, what are You saying to me through this lesson?

Mountains

FROM THE TEXT

This particular mountain was a situation I had been dealing with for years. I dealt with it in every way I knew how. But it just wouldn't change. It was like I wasn't speaking the right language. I couldn't explain myself. It was so frustrating.

It wasn't anything bad, just frustrating. I was tired of dealing with the same frustration over and over and over. I remember driving down the road, and thinking, *Okay, Lord, if it's that easy, then I'm going to do it.* So I spoke to that mountain, and said, *I want you to be removed, and I do not want to deal with this mountain anymore. Mountain be gone, be removed, be cast into the sea. This mindset is broken, it's gone, it's over.* And I tell you, it is the most wondrous thing that has ever happened, and it didn't even take a minute—immediately everything changed.

CONSIDER

Faith that moves mountains is complete faith in the Lord. It is a faith that knows He has the power and authority and He *can do* anything; nothing is impossible for Him. It is a faith that knows He cares about believers enough to care about the circumstances in their lives and believes that He *will do* it. And it is a faith that knows He loves YOU so much that He hears your prayers and responds to you, and He *will do it for you!*

SCRIPTURES

"...But if You can do anything, have compassion on us and help us." Jesus said to him, "If you can believe, all things are possible to him who believes." Immediately, the father of the child cried out and said with tears, "Lord, I believe; help my unbelief!" (Mark 9:22-24 NKJV)

So Jesus answered and said to them, "Have faith in God. For assuredly, I say to you, whoever says to this mountain, 'Be removed and be cast into the sea,' and does not doubt in his heart, but believes that those things he says will be done, he will have whatever he says. Therefore I say to you, whatever things you ask when you pray, believe that you receive them, and you will have them" (Mark 11:22-24 NKJV).

GOD-TALK

- Father, do You love me?
- Holy Spirit, what do You want to say to me about my faith?
- Jesus, will you show me any mountains that need to be removed from my life?

HEART-WORK

- Take time to remove the mountains from your soul and cast them into the sea.

- Ask the Holy Spirit to fill you and restore peace in your heart.

From your open, willing, and listening heart, **ask:**

Holy Spirit, what are You saying to me through this lesson?

Voice

FROM THE TEXT

The Lord told me He had given me a voice for women. His work was not only to save them, but He wanted to rebirth them. He wanted to give them back the life He created for them that had been taken from them. I'll never forget that day. I was in a strange country, away from all that was comfortable for me. In that place, I didn't have Troy, my brother, or my own mother to fall back on. I had Jesus.

I went to that place because of the mission I knew He had created for me. He used that to teach me that I will always need to stay close to Him because I can't possibly know all that He knows. He used me to set women free so they could find their own voice. All because I let Him give me mine.

CONSIDER

Jesus, in His infinite wisdom, called women to work in His ministry on earth. When Matthew records the genealogy down to Jesus's mother, Mary, he records four women: Tamar, Rahab, Ruth, Bathsheba—a revolutionary act in the culture of that day. The Gospels tell us of women who were not just present but actively involved in the early church. Their contributions, from Mary and Martha, Phoebe, Chloe, Priscilla, and so many others, are truly enlightening.

The longest conversation recorded in the Gospels that Jesus had was with a woman, the woman at the well. The outcome of that conversation was that *"Many Samaritans from the village believed in Jesus because the woman had said, 'He told me everything I ever did!'"* (John 4:39 NLT). Historians tell us her name was Photina; her work started a dynamic church there, and she became an evangelist.

God is still anointing women for work in His Kingdom. Give Him all of you, and watch what He will do through you!

SCRIPTURES

Jesus asked, "Who is my mother? Who are my brothers?" Then he pointed to his disciples and said, "Look, these are my mother and brothers. Anyone who does the will of my Father in heaven is my brother and sister and mother!" (Matthew 12:48-50 NLT).

God has given each of you a gift from his great variety of spiritual gifts. Use them well to serve one another. Do you have the gift of speaking? Then speak as though God himself were speaking through you. Do you have the gift of help-ing others? Do it with all the strength and energy that God supplies. Then, everything you do will bring glory to God through Jesus Christ. All glory and power to him forever and ever! Amen (1 Peter 4:10-11 NLT).

GOD-TALK

- Jesus, will You show me what You have given me to use in Your Kingdom?
- God, what do You want me to know that I don't know?

HEART-WORK

- Holy Spirit, will You show me any man-made doctrines I believe that aren't from You?
- Jesus, what do You want to transform in me?

From your open, willing, and listening heart, **ask:**

Holy Spirit, what are You saying to me through this lesson?

Moved by Grace

FROM THE TEXT

God began to lift grace off of me regarding children's ministry. What used to work didn't work anymore. I couldn't figure out what was going on; everything I had ever done and had been so successful with just wasn't working anymore. I kept praying and asking the Lord what was going on. I asked Him, "Why is this so hard now? Why are all these things that have been so great and so successful not working now?"

When Ron shared that message, he said, "The times in your life when God wants you to move and you don't want to move or you don't move, God will remove the grace He had always had on you that has allowed you to do what you have done. When that happens, it is definitely time for you to move."

CONSIDER

It is by God's grace that we have mindsets, skill sets, and "heart sets" to do ministry work with Him. He created us, and He has given us talents, IQs, abilities, or capabilities, so we should be grateful to Him for those attributes. He blesses us so we can be a blessing to others and advance His Kingdom. If He reassigns us, He will redirect the grace for all the things we need for that new assignment.

SCRIPTURES

And God is able to make all grace [every favor and earthly blessing] come in abundance to you, so that you may always [under all circumstances, regardless of the need] have complete sufficiency in everything [being completely self-sufficient in Him], and have an abundance for every good work and act of charity (2 Corinthians 9:8 Amplified Bible).

But by the grace of God I am what I am, and His grace toward me was not in vain; but I labored more abundantly than they all, yet not I, but the grace of God which was with me (1 Corinthians 15:10 NKJV).

GOD-TALK

- God, will You show me any place where I am outside Your perfect will for me?
- Are there any relationship connections that are not covered by Your grace to produce holy unions?
- Holy Spirit, what do You want to show me about the God-given grace in my life?

HEART-WORK

- Holy Spirit, search my heart and reveal any unholy unions I have formed that are hindering my ability to move with You into the perfect unions God has for me.
- Jesus, help me to do Your will in all areas of my life, and show me what I need to change.

From your open, willing, and listening heart, **ask:**

Holy Spirit, what are You saying to me through this lesson?

Good or God

FROM THE TEXT

I have sometimes developed relationships because I connected with people who I wanted to help or because I wanted to be nice or good to them. It is not always the Lord saying that He wants me to do that. Sometimes it's just me going before the Lord saying, "This is a good idea." But God sees they are in a different place in their journey, and it's not His idea. I might have messed up because I wasn't listening to the Holy Spirit. It is so important for us to listen to the Holy Spirit when we are making decisions. We can be led by our grace and our peace that comes from Him to know what works and what doesn't work.

CONSIDER

God is very relational, and He works through His people. The Bible tells us all the ways people worked together to accomplish great Kingdom good. When Jesus prayed just before He was crucified, He acknowledged that the Father had put the disciples and followers into His life. *"My prayer is not for the world, but for those you have given me because they belong to you. All who are mine belong to you, and you have given them to me, so they bring me glory"* (John 17:9-10 NLT).

God has a big, big ecclesia (church), but He calls us all to the right place at the right time. When we are developing relationships, we must seek Him first so we make *God* connections; not just *good* connections.

SCRIPTURES

The righteous should choose his friends carefully, for the way of the wicked leads them astray (Proverbs 12:26 NKJV).

There are "friends" who destroy each other, but a real friend sticks closer than a brother (Proverbs 18:24 NLT).

GOD-TALK

• Father, what do You want to say to me about the relationships in my life?

- Jesus, will You show me how to be a good friend who has good friends?

HEART-WORK

- Holy Spirit, reveal any unhealthy relationships I am attached to.
- Jesus, teach me how to hear You more clearly.

From your open, willing, and listening heart, **ask:**

Holy Spirit, what are You saying to me through this lesson?

Graceful Walk

FROM THE TEXT

So I start walking alongside the main highway. I'm frustrated and angry because I'm sure he is upset at me for not leaving the key in the car for him. I'm going over the whole thing in my head while walking along a busy road to the pharmacy. Then the Lord reminded me, "You have legs." And I said, "I do have legs." He said, "Grace walks that far every day with one hand, she has no legs, and she does not complain like you are." I felt the conviction of the Lord like I had never felt before.

It was in that moment that the Lord spoke to me again about grace. Not Grace the girl, but about the grace I needed to have in life for other people. And when He has called me to do something, to look at it in the right way, with the right perspective, from His point of view. I need to look at what I *do* have instead of what I don't have and be grateful for everything I have.

CONSIDER

Our outlook in life impacts our outcomes. We don't always get to choose the situations that happen in our life. We can, however, choose how we will walk through them. Scriptures point us to a life filled with gratitude and appreciation without complaining and criticizing. Jesus came to earth to fulfill the hardest mission ever given—and He did it while thanking God throughout the journey. He never complained. Oh, what a Savior!

SCRIPTURES

In everything give thanks, for this is the will of God in Christ Jesus for you (1 Thessalonians 5:18 NKJV).

You are my God, and I thank you. You are my God; I exalt you (Psalm 118:28 CJB).

Work hard to show the results of your salvation, obeying God with deep reverence and fear. For God is working in you, giving you the desire and the power to do what pleases him. Do everything without complaining and arguing so that no one can criticize you. Live clean, innocent lives as children of God, shining like bright lights in a world full of crooked and perverse people (Philippians 2:12-15 NLT).

GOD-TALK

- Take time to express your gratitude to God for all the ways He has shown up in your life; exalt Him, and love Him.

HEART-WORK

- Holy Spirit, reveal any negative, critical, complaining mindsets and "heart sets" in me.
- Lord, show me the root cause of each of those.
- Jesus, come heal the broken pieces and bring me freedom that can only come from You.
- Create a clean heart within me.

From your open, willing, and listening heart, **ask:**

Holy Spirit, what are You saying to me through this lesson?

Contented

FROM THE TEXT

Poverty is not just a financial state. It is a mindset, and it is a spirit of not having enough. My whole life, I have always had enough. I might not have had more than enough, but I have had enough.

The Lord showed me that the day would come when I would have an abundance. He said that I was solid in that place of poverty, so I wasn't going to mess up in that place of abundance.

CONSIDER

The poverty mindset focuses on the lack or limitations in a person's life. When lack is all a person can see, they will never see the possibilities available in what they do have. God wants us to appreciate and value what He has given us so He can entrust more to us.

When we think we don't have enough, we will fail to share what we have. God knows that when we share out of our "enough," He can trust us to share out of our "abundance."

SCRIPTURES

Keep your lives free from the love of money; and be satisfied with what you have; for God himself has said, "I will never fail you or abandon you" (Hebrews 13:5 CJB).

Not that I was ever in need, for I have learned how to be content with whatever I have. I know how to live on almost nothing or with everything. I have learned the secret of living in every situation, whether it is with a full stomach or empty, with plenty or little (Philippians 4:11-12 NLT).

GOD-TALK

- Holy Spirit, will You call to my remembrance the faithfulness of God's love for me?
- God, will You speak to me about what You have given me?
- Lord, have I been a good steward of all You have entrusted to me?
- Jesus, will You change my mindset to align with Your mind?

HEART-WORK

- Holy Spirit, will You reveal any place in my soul where I am insecure and speak to me about it?
- Will You show me where that came into my heart and speak Your truth over that situation?
- Lord, create a clean heart in me over all the financial situations in my life.

From your open, willing, and listening heart, **ask:**

Holy Spirit, what are You saying to me through this lesson?

Take Him at His Word

FROM THE TEXT

Luis believed. He believed what he was told—that he could have anything he wanted. And you know what? He came walking out of that shop with that wedding cake. The kids were hanging out the bus windows saying, "Oh, Luis, you're going to be in big trouble." He was just smiling, carrying this cake that was almost bigger than him, and he got on the bus. The kids were used to him being in trouble, so they were taunting him. Luis just looked at them and said, "The gringo said we could have whatever we want."

The whole scenario was such a faith builder for me, Troy, and our whole team. Whatever God says, He means it. You just have to believe it! Luis believed it. He didn't get that cake just for himself. As soon as he was settled on the bus, he shared it with all the other kids. When you believe what God says, and you take Him at His word, it isn't just for you—it's for everyone around you, too.

CONSIDER

The heart behind the work of SPARK is a reflection of God the Father's heart for His children. He is the good Father who wants to give each of us the desires of our hearts. When we take Him at His Word, we honor Him and show Him we appreciate His love and His goodness. He has exceedingly, abundantly more for us than we can imagine. Ask for the good things He has for you so you can share His goodness with the world around you. That brings Him great happiness.

SCRIPTURES

> *Now this is the confidence that we have in Him, that if we ask anything according to His will, He hears us. And if we know that He hears us, whatever we ask, we know that we have the petitions that we have asked of Him* (1 John 5:14-15 NKJV).

> *...your Father already knows your needs. Seek the Kingdom of God above all else, and he will give you everything you need. So don't be afraid, little flock. For it gives your Father great happiness to give you the Kingdom* (Luke 12:30-32 NLT).

GOD-TALK

- Holy Spirit, remind me of God's promises.

- Father, draw me closer to You.

- Jesus, what do You want to say to me about the Kingdom?

HEART-WORK

- Holy Spirit, reveal any lie I believe in my soul that is preventing me from having the confidence I need to ask the Father for what I need. Come, remove this from my soul.

- Father, will You show me how You see me?

From your open, willing, and listening heart, **ask:**

Holy Spirit, what are You saying to me through this lesson?

Keys

FROM THE TEXT

He gives you a key that will open a door that nobody else can close. But you have to use the key, you have to put it in the lock and unlock the door. Otherwise, it remains in your pocket, and you sit there whining and complaining. You are saying, "God, You have not answered my prayers. I've asked you, and you won't do this." Yet God is saying you have the key to this answer—it is in your pocket.

The key that Revelation is talking about is the anointing that David walked in. All of us have an anointing that we walk in. You can call it your superpower, but your anointing is the gifting within your life that seems normal to you.

CONSIDER

What's in your pocket? Has the Lord given you an anointing that you have tucked away? What has He given you that would bless so many others through Kingdom work? Have you found the door He wants to open? Are you ready to walk through the door that leads to the area of the Kingdom where He has called you?

SCRIPTURES

For by grace you have been saved through faith, and that not of yourselves; it is the gift of God, not of works, lest anyone should boast. For we are His workmanship, created in Christ Jesus for good works, which God prepared beforehand that we should walk in them (Ephesians 2:8-10 NKJV).

And I will give you the keys of the kingdom of heaven, and whatever you bind on earth will be bound in heaven, and whatever you loose on earth will be loosed in heaven (Matthew 16:19 NKJV).

GOD-TALK

- Father, speak to me about the anointing You have for me.
- Jesus, show me how to have a Kingdom mindset.
- Holy Spirit, will You give me a supernatural revelation about my place in the Kingdom?

HEART-WORK

- Holy Spirit, have Your way in my soul, renew my mind, heal my emotions, and bend my will to be the will of my Father.

From your open, willing, and listening heart, **ask:**

Holy Spirit, what are You saying to me through this lesson?

Seasons

FROM THE TEXT

I believe God is telling me that the coming season is going to look wildly different—not just for me but for the entire body of Christ. I am super excited about what He is going to do and what He is doing.

He also reminded me that I can't go on to the next chapter of life if I keep reading the last chapter over and over. You have to go from old to new, old wineskin to new wineskin, because He is doing a new thing.

CONSIDER

Ecclesiastes 3 tells us that there is a season for every purpose under Heaven. Just like in the natural world there are seasons of fall, winter, spring, and summer, and we adjust our lives to walk in them appropriately. We wear boots in winter and flip-flops in summer; our activities are based on the conditions around us in the natural. We must listen carefully to God so we are ready to participate with Him in the new things He is going to do.

SCRIPTURES

And no one puts new wine into old wineskins; or else the new wine bursts the wineskins, the wine is spilled, and the wineskins are ruined. But new wine must be put into new wineskins (Mark 2:22 NKJV).

GOD-TALK AND HEART-WORK

Enter into a conversation with God and ask the Holy Spirit to work in your soul as you prayerfully read through Ecclesiastes chapter 3 (NKJV), listening for what He wants to say to you.

> *To everything there is a season,*
>
> *A time for every purpose under heaven:*
>
> *A time to be born, and a time to die;*
>
> *A time to plant, and a time to pluck what is planted;*
>
> *A time to kill, and a time to heal;*
>
> *A time to break down, and a time to build up;*
>
> *A time to weep, and a time to laugh;*
>
> *A time to mourn, and a time to dance;*
>
> *A time to cast away stones, and a time to gather stones;*
>
> *A time to embrace, and a time to refrain from embracing;*
>
> *A time to gain, and a time to lose;*
>
> *A time to keep, and a time to throw away;*
>
> *A time to tear, and a time to sew;*
>
> *A time to keep silence, and a time to speak;*
>
> *A time to love, and a time to hate;*
>
> *A time of war, and a time of peace.*

From your open, willing, and listening heart, **ask:**

> *Holy Spirit, what are You saying to me through this lesson?*

Kingdomized

FROM THE TEXT

Kingdomized is such good language, because when you have an encounter with Jesus, He doesn't leave you the same. You don't look the same, you don't act the same. You now have a vision and a hope for the future that you never had.

He doesn't leave us the same way as when He found us. When Jesus healed people, they were no longer in need of healing. They were healed. They could walk, they could run, they could dance, they could see, and do all sorts of amazing feats. When Jesus forgave their sins, they were no longer sinners. When you see someone after they accepted salvation, all of a sudden the person looks different. An inner joy shines through that shows on their face. That is what transformation is. That is what the Kingdom is. That's what we are supposed to do as representatives of Jesus Himself.

CONSIDER

How are you different since you became a believer? Have you been radically transformed? Your testimony will help others want Jesus, too.

More than that, though, your experience with Jesus should have given you Kingdomized eyesight. Do you see people the way Jesus sees them and treat them with the love and compassion He did? He wants us to go into all the world and represent Him. We must be Kingdomized to do that well.

SCRIPTURES

*Don't copy the behavior and customs of this world, but **let God transform you into a new person** by changing the way you think. Then you will learn to know God's will for you, which is good and pleasing and perfect* (Romans 12:2 NLT).

Then Jesus said to those Jews who believed Him, "If you abide in My word, you are My disciples indeed. And you shall know the truth, and the truth shall make you free" (John 8:31-32 NKJV).

GOD-TALK

- Today, draw near to Jesus and rest in His love, letting His presence immerse you in Kingdom visions that flow from His heart.

HEART-WORK

- Holy Spirit, come wash the worldly remnants out of my soul.

From your open, willing, and listening heart, **ask:**

Holy Spirit, what are You saying to me through this lesson?

SPARK Speaks

Home is more than a building.
Home is a hope and a future.

Think about all the people around the world whose house is made of grass or mud with a leaky roof. Having a home is such a blessing. To the kids that we rescue, having a home is safety; it is family. I love how Jesus loves children. Kids believe you; they trust you. Don't walk past kids who need you; Jesus never walked past. Having a home means everything to these children—not only to have a home, but somewhere to be safe and to have a family.

SPARK offers hope and gives them a chance to be children. Our goal is to get vulnerable and hurting kids into situations where they can grow and thrive and prosper. A place where they are protected and blessed and loved.

SPARK is a sanctuary, a safe place. The kids in our program have literally had their lives saved. Jesus has a heart for these kids. He says do not shoo them away from Me. His Kingdom looks like these kids. It's a happy place.

We rescue children, bring them into the body of Christ, teach them about Jesus, and show them the love of Jesus. We urge you to watch how these kids will reach other kids and they will reach even more kids—ones we are unable to reach.

My people will live in peaceful dwelling places, in secure homes, in undisturbed places of rest (Isaiah 32:18 New International Version).

We continue to rescue kids, bring them to Jesus, and give them hope. The real-life story told in the movie *Sound of Freedom* was set in the country of Colombia, in the area where SPARK headquarters are located. In the movie, a determined ex-federal agent traveled up a river and rescued a little girl from a dangerous drug cartel. That is where we are rescuing children as well. We have a home full of those kids who were captured and used and abused in that region.

This generation is holding hands with the next generation and bringing up rescuers. There are many untold stories of this inhuman cycle of brutality, but the stories we do know represent those children, too. Some people still say that sex trafficking doesn't exist—meanwhile we have the terrible privilege of looking into these children's eyes, knowing it does indeed exist, and then rescuing them.

When you help rescue these kids, you are reaching out and taking their hands and giving them hope. We hold their hands and walk them to a place of nurture and safety. They hold your hand like no one has ever held your hand before. The desperate way they hold on says, "Please don't let go of me. Please let me stay here forever." We have to say, "Yes, we are going to hold your hand until you feel safe."

Watching these kids' lives transform is truly watching a miracle unfold. We have many stories to tell, and each one is more awe-inspiring than the one before. One group is truly remarkable that I want to share with you.

THE RESCUED BECOME RESCUERS

This group of young men came to us as young boys. We raised them, and they became family. They are in their mid-twenties now. One is a lawyer, one is in training to be a heart surgeon, one is a big machinery operator, and one is a pastor. They all regularly go to the villages and support the kids in a variety of ways. The school fees are paid and they provide the kids' uniforms and classroom supplies. This group of young men have told us they do what we taught them to do while growing up in our home—they take what they have and sow it into other kids.

Because their lives were changed, it is important to all of them to help change other kids' lives.

They came together and formed a soccer team comprised of young men from different religions including Muslim, Christian, and other faiths. However, to be on the team, the players have to participate in a Bible study. They evangelize while having fun and fellowshipping. The team is really, really good, so everybody wants to be on this SPARK team.

Jesus said to go into all the world and make disciples. The word *disciple* means "learner," and these young men are teachers to the world. They are teaching by their actions as they give, encourage, and include others. When others see the joy that is so evident in this group of guys' lives, it "sparks" something in their hearts to want it, too.

Early Kankoola Area   First Picture of the Uganda Land

Kankoola Water Well

Leanna in the Amazon

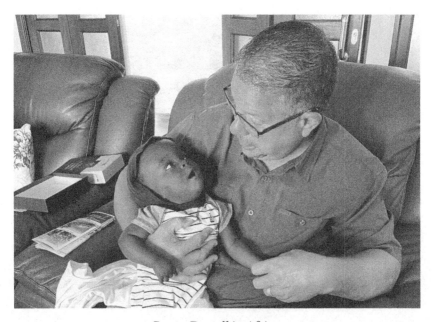

Pastor Darrell in Africa

Leanna with Pastor Darrell

Lisa and Leanna in Uganda

Uganda

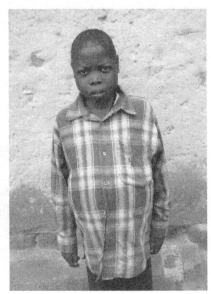

Jimmy

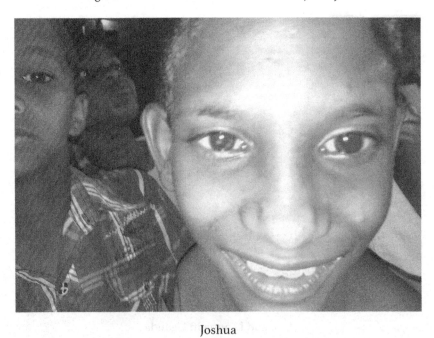

Joshua

Leanna and Team at Wailing Wall in Israel

Elanna from Israel   Leanna and Queen Best

Leanna and Grace

Leanna Spark Picture

SPARK Soccer Team

About Leanna Brewer

LEANNA BREWER is the cofounder of OpenDoor Church, and the OpenDoor food bank, and she is the founder of SPARK WORLDWIDE.

She has been and currently is responsible for feeding untold numbers of people worldwide and housing thousands of orphans. Leanna has traveled to more than 50 countries, digging fresh-water wells, preaching the Gospel and Serving, Protecting And Raising Kids, which is the acronym for SPARK.

Leanna has authored several children's books and hosts a weekly podcast. She serves on staff at OpenDoor Church as the women's pastor and co-senior pastor with her husband of 35 years, Troy Brewer. Leanna is the mother of four and the grandmother of seven.

CONTACT INFORMATION

OpenDoor Church

and

SPARK Worldwide

329 S Dobson Street
Burleson, TX 76028
Phone: 817-295-7671

Website: opendoorexperience.com

info@sparkworldwide.org

YOUR
Prophetic
COMMUNITY

Sign up for a **FREE** subscription to the Destiny Image digital magazine and get awesome content delivered directly to your inbox!

destinyimage.com/signup

Sign up for Cutting-Edge Messages that Supernaturally Empower You

- Gain valuable insights and guidance based on biblical principles
- Deepen your faith and understanding of God's plan for your life
- Receive regular updates and prophetic messages
- Connect with a community of believers who share your values and beliefs

Experience Fresh Video Content that Reveals Your Prophetic Inheritance

- Receive prophetic messages and insights
- Connect with a powerful tool for spiritual growth and development
- Stay connected and inspired on your faith journey

Listen to Powerful Podcasts that Propel You into God's Presence Every Day

- Deepen your understanding of God's prophetic assignment
- Experience God's revival power throughout your day
- Learn how to grow spiritually in your walk with God

Made in the USA
Monee, IL
21 February 2025

12700139R00154